neglected instrumentalists

adrian aeschbacher
eduard erdmann
conrad hansen
ludwig hoelscher
georg kulenkampff
enrico mainardi
carl seemann
max strub
gerhard taschner
friedrich wührer

discographies compiled by john hunt

Neglected Instrumentalists

Adrian Aeschbacher, Eduard Erdmann,
Conrad Hansen, Ludwig Hoelscher,
Georg Kulenkampff, Enrico Mainardi,
Carl Seemann, Max Strub,
Gerhard Taschner, Friedrich Wührer

John Hunt

© John Hunt 2020

ISBN 978-1-901395-37-2

Travis & Emery Music Bookshop
17 Cecil Court
London
WC2N 4EZ
United Kingdom.
Tel. (+44) (0) 20 7240 2129.
newpublications@travis-and-emery.com

Contents

Introduction/*page 5*
Adrian Aeschbacher/*page 11*
Eduard Erdmann/*page 21*
Conrad Hansen/*page 33*
Ludwig Hoelscher/*page 47*
Georg Kulenkampff/*page 61*
Enrico Mainardi/*page 87*
Carl Seemann/*page 105*
Max Strub/*page 123*
Gerhard Taschner/*page 133*
Friedrich Wührer/*page 143*
Index of repertoire/*page 159*

Neglected instrumentalists: an introduction

Classical record catalogues from the middle of last century reveal a plethora of performances in all the main genres, not least in the field of chamber and instrumental music. Nowhere was this activity more concentrated than in the German-speaking countries, with a high level of work emerging on Grammophon, Telefunken and Electrola labels. From the mid 1930s, of course, performers of Jewish origin were obliged to leave their homeland and to pursue their careers, to great acclaim, outside of Germany. The work of those performing artists left behind has, in my view, received less attention than it deserves

From certain quarters of the critical fraternity emerges the rather cynical suggestion that these artists may not have been given so much exposure by the record companies if their Jewish colleagues had remained: I feel that such an assertion is entirely unjustified, not least in the light of the evidence documented in these ten discographies. In almost all cases we are dealing with instrumentalists who accommodated themselves, to varying degrees, with the National Socialist regime. Yet I can find no serious evidence that they voluntarily participated in any political activity, with the result that they could soon resume work after 1945 and make some of their last recordings for the emerging LP medium. Alongside and subsequent to their concert and recording careers, these performers held teaching posts at the various prestigious German conservatories.

introduction/continued

The Swiss-born pianist **Adrian Aeschbacher** (1912-2002) is probably best known to record collectors through his two collaborations (live concert recordings) with the conductor Wilhelm Furtwangler: Brahms Second Piano Concerto in Berlin (1943) and Beethoven First Piano Concerto in Lucerne (1947). Although apparently he had a predilection for contemporary Swiss composers, Aeschbacher's recorded legacy centres round the music of Schubert and Schumann, a collection of the latter's solo piano recordings for Deutsche Grammophon in the 1950s having been published on CD by KASP Records. His main teaching activity took place between 1965 and 1977 at the Musikhochschule in the German city of Saarbrücken.

Eduard Erdmann (1896-1958) was also a regular concert collaborator with Furtwängler between 1922 and 1940, but sadly none of those performances were recorded. Indeed, Erdmann appears to have been a reluctant recording artist (although he did visit the Abbey Road studios for one Parlophone session in 1935). It is only due to the enterprise of the various post-war West German radio stations that we have multiple versions of Erdmann performing, among others, the music of Schubert and Reger, with both of whom he seems to have had a special affinity. Hamburg's music conservatory became the main centre of his teaching work in the decade beore his death.

introduction/continued

Conrad Hansen (1906-2002) was accepted as early as 1922 as a student of the renowned pianist Edwin Fischer, whom he went on to assist with teaching duties at the Berlin Musikhochschule. After the Second War he formed a piano trio with the violinist Erich Röhn and cellist Arthur Troester, as well as being a co-founder of the Detmold Music Academy. Plans to record the complete Mozart Sonatas on fortepiano for Deutsche Grammophon in the 1950s did not come to fruition, however a few of those sonatas which were recorded can now be heard in the CD-set *Deutsxhe Grammophon: the Mono era 1948-1957 (catalogue number 479 5516).*

One of the most extensively recorded of our instrumentalists was the German cellist **Ludwig Hoelscher** (1907-1996), embracing concerti, chamber music and a long-standing duo with the pianist Elly Ney: their major achievement probably being the complete works for cello and piano by Beethoven. Other eminent soloiss with whom Hoelscher collaborated include violinist Gerhard Taschner and pianist Walter Gieseking.

To **Georg Kulenkampff** (1898-1948) fell the honour of belatedly premiering the Schumann Violin Concerto, both in concert and in the recording studio: that studio recording was just one of a long line of concerto performances for the Telefunken label. In some critical quarters Kulenkampff is reproached for having set down so many of what we would call salon pieces: in order to counter such a charge, Kulenkampff scholar Wolfgang Wendel has assembled those recordings for a CD project entitled *Podium Legenda,*

introduction/continued

which takes in almost the violinist's entire output, right up to the final sessions for Decca with the young Georg Solti at the piano.

Italian-born **Enrico Mainardi** (1897-1976) studied cello both in Milan and Berlin before coming to the attention of conductor Erich Kleiber, who recruited him as principal to the Dresden Philharmonie and subsequently the Berlin Staatskapelle, during which time he recorded the solo cello part in *Don Quixote* under its composer's direction. Mainardi continued to be a favoured soloist in Germany during the years of the Third Reich, and after the war formed a trio with pianist Edwin Fischer and violinist Kulenkampff (replaced after the latter's death by Wolfgang Schneiderhan). All of Mainardi's recordings for the company have been assembled as a 14-CD set by Deutshe Grammophon in South Korea.

Carl Seemann (1910-1983) was another German pianist who deserves better recognition: the only significant re-issue among his many records for Deutsche Grammophon appears to be the complete solo piano music of Mozart (CD 477 5856). Specially notable among other recordings is the extensive partnership with Wolfgang Schneiderhan (violin sonatas by Mozart, Beethoven and Brahms, among others).

introduction/continued

Violinist **Max Strub** (1900-1966) recorded almost exclusively as a chamber music player, his only major outing as a concerto soloist being the Beethoven Violin Concerto wit Karl Böhm and the Dresden Staatskapelle for Electrola in 1939. Strub's own string quartet numbered, at different times, a host of distinguished soloists as its members, including Josef Krips. Walter Trampler and Ludwig Hoelscher.

Gerhard Taschner (1922-1976) was appointed by Wilhelm Furtwängler to be Konzertmeister of the Berlin Philharmonic when he was only nineteen years old, a position he held until the end of the war. At the same time he was already appearing as an outstanding soloist, but made surprisingy few gramophone recordings. And so, as in the case of pianist Eduard Erdmann, it is thanks to the enterprising post-war West German radio stations that so many of Taschner's brilliant concerto performances are preserved (Beethoven, Bruch, Fortner, Hindemith, Mendelssohn, Pfitzner, Tchaikovsky).

The Vienna-based pianist **Friedrich Wührer** (1900-1975) was an advocate of much contemporary music in his early career, but is now mainly remembered for his post-war association with the Vox record label, for which he performed a wide range of repertoire, perhaps most notably the first complete traversal on record of the Schubert Piano Sonatas.

introduction/concluded

As far as 78rpm recordings are concerned, matrix numbers are given in the left-hand column (two numbers making up the two sides of each disc), with the disc's catalogue number following in a second column.

Having referred in these introductory notes to a number of other artists who collaborated in chamber music recordings, I should point out that I have already documented the work of at least two of them: Elly Ney in the volume *Pianists for the connoisseur (ISBN 1 901395 12 X)* and Wolfgang Schneiderhan in the volume *Great Violinists (ISBN 901395 18 9)*.

In compiling the discographies I have to thank the following, who have supplied information: Roderick Krüsemann, Alan Newcombe, Tully Potter and Wolfgang Wendel.

John Hunt 2019

ADRIAN AESCHBACHER pianist 1912-2002

<u>20-30 september 1940/grammophon sessions in berlin alte-jakob-strasse studios</u>
schubert four impromptus D899
8622   LM 67 977
8623
8624   LM 67 978
8625
8626   LM 67 979
8627
schubert four impromptus D935
8628   LM 67 980
8629
8630   LM 67 981
8631
8632   LM 67 982
8633
8634   LM 67 983
8635

<u>13 december 1940/grammophon session in berlin alte-jakob-strasse studios</u>
handel chaconne in g
1118   LM 67 650
1119

1 april 1942/grammophon sessions in berlin
alte-jakob-strasse studios
schubert trout quintet D667
with members of the hanke string quartet
1788   LM 67 842
1789
1790   LM 67 843
1791
1792   LM 67 844
1793
1794   LM 67 845
1795
1796   LM 67 846
1797

22 march 1943/grammophon sessions in
berlin alte-jakob-strasse studios
haydn piano trio in g
with max strub, violin/gaspar cassado. cello
2300   LM 68 383
2301
2302   LM 68 384
2304

7 june 1943/grammophon sessions in berlin
alte-jakob-strasse studios
schubert moments musicaux D780

1737	LM 67 751
1738	
1739	LM 67 752
2217	
1816	LM 67 753
2216	
2218	LM 67 754
1776	

12-15 december 1943/reichsrundfunk concert
recording in berlin philharmonie
brahms piano concerto no 2 in b flat op 83
with philharmonisches orchester berlin/
wilhelm furtwängler
lp: melodiya M10 45921 009/french
furtwängler society SWF 8502
cd: french furtwängler society SWF 951-952/
music and arts CD 941/dante LYS 049/
tahra FURT 1004-1007/FURT 1038-1039/
berliner philharmoniker BPHR 180 181/
chibas restorations 1109

5 april 1944/reichsrundfunk recording in
hamburg sendesaal
**brahms piano trio in c op 87; mozart andante
and allegretto from piano trio in g K564**
with max strub, piano/gaspar cassado, cello
cd: meloclassic MC 3001

31 may 1944/grammophon session in berlin
schubert impromptu D935 no 2
2212   LM 68 098
2213

10 october 1945/swiss radio recording in lausanne theatre municipal
bach concerto for three pianos BWV 1063
with paul baumgartner, piano/edwin fischer, piano/chamber orchestra
unpublished

27 august 1947/swiss radio concert recording in luzern kunsthaus
beethoven piano concerto no 1 in c op 15
with schweizerisches festspielorchester/
wilhelm furtwängler
lp: rococo 2106/french furtwängler society
SWF 7401/japan JPL 1006/discocorp RR 205/
RR 438/nippon columbia OZ 7595
cd: french furtwängler society SWF 961-962/
dante LYS 199/elaborations ELA 006/
music and arts CD 839/CD 1018/
tahra FURT 1028-1029

aeschbacher

19 september 1950/deutsche grammophon sessions
in hamburg
**beethoven piano sonata no 17 in d minor op 31 no 2
"tempest"; rondo capriccioso op 120**
2142   LVM 72 026
2143
2144   LVM 72 027
2145
45: EPL 30 323 (rondo)
lp: LPM 18 220 (sonata)
cd: crq editions CRQCD 054-055
brahms rhapsodies op 79 nos 1 and 2
2193   LVM 72 051
2078
45: EPL 30 242
cd: crq editions CRQCD 054-055
beethoven rondo in c op 51 no 1
45: EPL 30 323
cd: crq editions CRQCD 054-055

23-27 may 1951/deutsche grammophon sessions
in hannover beethovensaal
schumann davidsbündlertänze
lp: LP 16 016
cd: kasp recordings KASP 57671
**beethoven piano sonata no 26 in e flat
op 81a "les adieux"**
lp: LPM 18 220
cd: crq editions CRQCD 054-055

2-4 august 1951/deutsche grammophon sessions
in munich gaiselgasteig
schumann drei romanzen op 28
2784   LVM 72 060
2317
lp: LP 16 121/LPE 17 082
cd: kasp recordings KASP 57671/
crq editions CRQCD 054-055
beethoven ecossaise in e flat; für elise
45: NL 32 031
cd: crq editions CRQCD 054-055

14-21 january 1952/deutsche grammophon
sessions in berlin jesus-christus-kirche
brahms piano concerto no 2 in b flat op 83
with philharmonisches orchester berlin/
paul van kempen
3388   LVM 72 177
3389
3390   LVM 72 178
3391
3392   LVM 72 179
3393
3394   LVM 72 180
3395
lp: LPM 18 024
cd: 479 5516/tahra TAH 512-513

1-11 november 1952/deutsche grammophon
sessions in hannover beethovensaal
schubert trout quintet D667
with members of the koeckert string quartet
4193   LVM 72 300
4198
4194   LVM 72 301
3197
4195   LVM 72 302
4196
schubert moments musicaux D780
lp: LPE 17 090/LPM 18 213
cd: kasp recordings KASP 57671

16-18 february 1953/deutsche grammophon
sessions in hannover beethovensaal
schubert wanderer fantasy D790
4596   LVM 72 372
4597
4598   LVM 72 373
4599
lp: LPM 18 213
schubert piano sonata in b flat D960
lp: LPM 18 139
schumann album für die jugend op 68
45: NL 32 233

2-3 march 1953/deutsche grammophon sessions
in berlin jesus-christus-kirche
grieg piano concerto in a minor op 16
with philharmonisches orchester berlin/
leopold ludwig
4570   LVM 72 410
4571
4572   LVM 72 411
4573
lp: LP 16 075/LPE 17 143/89 521/2870 122

24 april 1953/deutsche grammophon session
in hannover beethovensaal
schumann kinderszenen op 15
lp: LP 16 121/LPE 17 082
cd: crq editions CRQCD 054-055

aeschbacher

<u>22-24 september 1953/deutsche grammophon sessions in hannover beethovensaal</u>

schubert four impromptus D899

5037   LVM 72 416
5038
5039   LVM 72 417
5040

lp: LP 16 115

schubert four impromptus D935

lp: LP 16 116

<u>12 march 1956/deutsche grammophon sessions in hannover beethovensaal</u>

schumann toccata op 7; arabeske op 18; blumenstück op 19; waldszenen op 82

lp: LPEM 19 079
cd: crq editions CRQCD 054-055

EDUARD ERDMANN pianist 1896-1958

<u>1920s/duo-art piano roll</u>
glazunov nocturne op 37
cd: bayer 200 044-045

<u>1928/grammophon sessions in berlin</u>
erdmann foxtrot in c; krenek kleine suite
940   95108
941
cd: bayer 200 044-045
tiessen die amsel; ein sperling in die hand des eduard erdmann
944   95109
945
cd: bayer 200 044-045
smetana hochzeitsszenen nos 1 and 2
1439   90023
1440
cd: bayer 200 044-045
debussy preludes: minstrels from book 1; ondine from book 2
1441   90024
1442
cd: bayer 200 044-045

<u>22 september 1932/grossdeutscher rundfunk recording in berlin</u>
debussy fantaisie pour piano et orchestre
with berliner funkorchester/bruno seidler-winkler
unpublished and probably incomplete

<u>7 september 1935/parlophone session in london abbey road studios</u>
brahms intermezzi op 117 nos 1 and 2
CXE 7151   E 11287/odeon 0-6972/decca (usa) 25326
CXE 7152
beethoven bagatelle op 126 no 6; brahms intermezzo op 117 no 3
CXE 7153   E 11295/odeon 0-6995/decca (usa) 25783
CXE 7154

7 november 1935/telefunken sessions in berlin
singakademie
beethoven piano concerto no 3 in c minor op 37
with philharmonisches orchester berlin/
artur rother

20976	E 1889/ultraphon F 22546
20977	
20978	E 1890/ultraphon F 22547
20979	
20980	E 1891/ultraphon F 22548
20981	
20982	E 1892/ultraphon F 22549
20983	

cd: tahra TAH 199-200/classico PTC 2002/
bayer 200 044-045

27 january 1937/reichsrundfunk recording in
berlin haus des rundfunks
mozart piano concerto in d minor K466
with orchester des reichssenders berlin/
heinrich steiner
unpublished

4 january 1938/reichsrundfunk recording in hamburg
mozart piano concerto in c minor K491
with orchester des reichssenders hamburg/
eigel kruttge
unpublished

18 november 1940/grammophon sessions in berlin alte-jakob-strasse studios
haydn variations in f minor
1509   67 727
1510
1511   67 728
45: EPL 30 410
lp: 419 1631/emi F699.314163
cd: bayer 200 044-045
schubert zwölf deutsche tänze D790
1512   68 281
1513
lp: 419 1631
cd: 483 6145/bayer 200 044-045

1943/reichsrundfunk recording in berlin haus des rundfunks
debussy fantaisie pour piano et orchestre
with grosses orchester des berliner rundfunks/
hans rosbaud
cd: tahra TAH 199-200

1944/reichsrundfunk recording in hamburg
schubert piano sonata in a D959
cd: tahra TAH 386-387

17 january 1945/reichsrundfunk recording in munich
schumann konzertstück op 92
with orchester des reichssenders münchen/
hans rosbaud
lp: vox PLP 1700/TV 12437
cd: bayer 200 044-045/tahra TAH 199-200
vox editions incorrectly named conductor as gustav görlich

april-june 1946/nordwestdeutscher rundfunk recordings in hamburg
milhaud piano sonata; schoenberg sechs klavierstücke op 19
unpublished

4 november 1948/hessischer rundfunk recordings
in frankfurt-am-main
handel keyboard suite no 4
cd: tahra TAH 199-200
liszt valse oubliee no 1; mephisto polka
cd: tahra TAH 386-387

20 april 1949/nordwestdeutscher rundfunk
recording in hamburg
schubert piano sonata in a D664
lp: electrola E 80996/WCLP 951/F669.214163

2 may 1949/süddeutscher rundfunk recordings
in stuttgart
beethoven piano concerto no 3 in c minor op 37
with sinfonie-orchester des süddeutschen
rundfunks/hans müller-kray
cd: tahra TAH 386-387
schubert piano sonata in a D664
unpublished

<u>18 april 1950/westdeutscher rundfunk recording in köln funkhaus</u>
schumann sechs intermezzi op 4; schubert piano sonata in b flat D960
cd: orfeo C722 071B
w.f. bach four polonaises
unpublished

<u>17-18 may and *12 december 1950/norddeutscher rundfunk recordings in hamburg</u>
schubert piano sonata in c minor D958
lp: electrola E 80947/WCLP 958/F669.214163
schubert moment musical D780 no 3; impromptu D935 no 2; *stephen heller preludes op 15
unpublished

<u>17 january 1951/radio bremen recording</u>
schubert piano sonata in b flat D960
cd: tahra TAH 386-387

<u>19 march 1951/westdeutscher rundfunk recording in köln funkhaus</u>
reger piano concerto in f minor
with sinfonie-orchester des westdeutschen rundfunks/hans rosbaud
cd: orfeo C722 071B

<u>25 march 1951/norddeutscher rundfunk recordings in hamburg</u>
schumann fantasiestücke op 12; schubert piano sonatas in a D664 and c minor D958
unpublished

<u>3 october 1951/hessischer rundfunk recording in frankfurt-am-main</u>
reger piano concerto in f minor
with sinfonie-orchester des hessischen rundfunks/ herbert albert
unpublished

<u>12 december 1951/norddeutscher rundfunk recordings in hamburg</u>
schumann fantasiestücke op 12
lp: electrola E 80948/WCLP 959/1C053 28947/ F669.214163
beethoven piano sonata in e minor op 90; byrd will you walk through the wood?
unpublished

17 march 1952/bayerischer rundfunk recordings
in munich
mussorgsky pictures at an exhibition
cd: tahra TAH 199-200
schubert piano sonata In b flat D960
cd: tahra TAH 218-219
schubert piano sonata in b D575
unpublished

22 april 1952/radio bremen recordings
schumann impromptu on themes of clara wieck; mozart piano sonata K533/K494
cd: tahra TAH 386-387

16 november 1952/süddeutscher rundfunk recordings in stuttgart villa berg
beethoven piano concerto no 3 in c minor op 37; schumann konzertstück op 92
with sinfonie-orchester des süddeutschen rundfunks/hans müller-kray
cd: swr music SWR 10203
weber piano concerto no 1 op 11
with sinfonie-orchester des süddeutschen rundfunks/hans müller-kray
unpublished

<u>19 november 1952/hessischer rundfunk recording in frankfurt-am-main</u>
beethoven piano concerto no 3 in c minor op 37
with sinfonie-orchester des hessischen rundfunks/ kurt schröder
unpublished

<u>6 january 1953/hessischer rundfunk recordings in frankfurt-am-main</u>
schubert piano sonata in g D894
cd: tahra TAH 218-219
beethoven piano sonata in c minor op 13 "pathetique"
unpublished

<u>21 may 1953/norddeutscher rundfunk recordings in hamburg</u>
schubert piano sonata in b flat D960
lp: electrola E 80947/WCLP 958/F669.214163
schubert four impromptus D899
lp: electrola E 80948/WCLP 959/F669.214163
schubert allegretto in c minor D915
unpublished

<u>28 february-2 march 1954/bayerischer rundfunk recordings in munich</u>
schubert piano sonatas in d D958 and c minor D959
cd: tahra TAH 218-219
reger piano concerto in f minor
with münchner philharmoniker/fritz rieger
unpublished

<u>19 may 1954/norddeutscher rundfunk recordings in hamburg</u>
mussorgsky pictures at an exhibition; schubert four impromptus   D935
unpublished

<u>30 may 1954/norddeutscher rundfunk recording in hamburg</u>
beethoven piano concerto no 5 in e flat op 73 "emperor"
with sinfonie-orchester des norddeutschen rundfunks/hans schmidt-isserstedt
unpublished
according to rene tremine the tapes of this recording were probably erased

<u>2 december 1954/bayerischer rundfunk recording in munich</u>
weber piano concerto no 1 op 11
with münchner philharmoniker/fritz rieger
unpublished

17 may 1956/norddeutscher rundfunk recording in hamburg
schubert piano sonata in a D959
lp: electrola E 80946/WCLP 957/F669.214163

CONRAD HANSEN pianist 1906-2002

<u>1932/electrola sessions in berlin</u>
bach concerto for three pianos BWV1064
with edwin fischer, piano/käthe aschaffenburg, piano/ fischer chamber orchestra

OD 1495	unpublished
OD 1496	
OD 1497	unpublished
OD 1498	
OD 1499	unpublished
OD 1500	
OD 1501	unpublished
OD 1502	

8-11 july 1940/telefunken magnetophon sessions
in berlin philharmonie
tchaikovsky piano concerto no 1 in b flat minor op 23
with philharmonisches orchester berlin/
willem mengelberg

25083	SK 3092/ultraphon G 14273
25084	
25085	SK 3093/ultraphon G 14274
25086	
25087	SK 3094/ultraphon G 14275
25088	
25089	SK 3095/ultraphon G 14276

lp: capitol P 8097/past masters PM 18
cd: 844 160/243 7262/biddulph WHL 051/
dante LYS 239/pristine audio PASC 348/
warner (japan) WQCC 351-354

22-23 june 1941/telefunken sessions in berlin
singakademie
beethoven piano concerto no 5 in e flat
op 73 "emperor"
with orchester der städtischen oper/eugen jochum

25901	SK 3203
25902	
25903	SK 3204
25904	
25905	SK 3205
25906	
25907	SK 3206
25908	
25909	SK 3207
25910	

27 june-4 july 1941/telefunken sessions in berlin singakademie

mozart piano concerto in d K537 "coronation"
with orchester der städtischen oper/artur rother

25939	SK 3734
25940	
25941	SK 3735
25942	
25943	SK 3736
25944	
25945	SK 3737
25946	

liszt piano concerto no 1 in e flat
with orchester der städtischen oper/artur rother

25968	unpublished
25969	
25970	unpublished
25971	
25972	unpublished

20-21 july 1942/telefunken sessions in berlin
brahms ballade op 118 no 5; franck prelude fugue et chorale

26565   SK 3741
26566
26567   SK 3742
26568

mozart piano sonata in g K283; rondo in d K485

26570   SK 3724
26571
26572   SK 3725
26589

brahms intermezzo op 117 no 7; chopin nocturne op 9 no 2

26573   unpublished
26574

<u>31 october-3 november 1943/reichsrundfunk
concert recording in berlin philharmonie</u>
beethoven piano concerto no 4 in g op 58
with philharmonisches orchester berlin/
wilhelm furtwängler
lp: unicorn UNI 105/french furtwängler society
SWF 7005R/nippon columbia DXM 104/deutsche
grammophon 2535 807/melodiya M10 46067 003/
emi 3C153 53010-53016M
cd: melodiya MEL 10 00771/russian compact disc
RCD 25002/french furtwängler society SWF 941/
arkadia CDWFE 365/music and arts CD 839/
tahra FURT 1034-1035/chibas restorations 1101/
berliner philharmoniker BPHR 180 181

<u>1943/reichsrundfunk recording in berlin
haus des rundfunks</u>
beethoven piano concerto no 3 in c minor op 37
with grosses orchester des berliner rundfunks/
artur rother
lp: regent MG 5026
*published under pseudonyms franz schulz/berlin
symphony orchestra/gustav kuntz*

1944/reichsrundfunk recording in berlin haus des rundfunks
reger movements from deutsche tänze für vier hände
with a. janowski, second piano
unpublished

10 april 1952/rias berlin concert recording in titania palest
beethoven piano concerto no 5 in e flat op 73 "emperor"
with rias-sinfonie-orchester/karl böhm
cd: musicaphon M 56845

19-20 april 1953/rias berlin concert recording in titania palest
brahms piano concerto no 1 in d minor op 15
with rias-sinfonie-orchester/ferenc fricsay
lp: longanesi GCL 50/nomos 980 9212

22 may 1953/bayericher rundfunk recordings in munich
beethoven piano sonatas in c minor op 10 no 1 and in c minor op 111; brahms piano sonata no 3 and intermezzo op 119 no 1
cd: musicaphon M 36845

<u>15 august 1953/rias berlin recording</u>
tchaikovsky piano concerto no 1 in b flat minor op 23
with rias-sinfonie-orchester/wolfgang sawallisch
lp: remington R 199-197/masterseal MSLP 5006/ bertelsmann 13174/deutscher schallplattenring DSCC 67/eurodisc GK 60116
further sessions held in february 1954

<u>14-16 september 1954/telefunken sessions in hamburg-harburg</u>
schubert piano trio in e flat D939
with erich röhn, violin/arthur troester, cello
lp: LE 6525/LGX 66019/BLE 14131
schubert notturno D897
with erich röhn, violin/arthur troester, cello
unpublished

<u>8-11 december 1954/telefunken sessions in berlin lichterfelder festsäle</u>
dvorak piano trio in e minor op 90 "dumky"
with erich röhn, violin/arthur troester, cello
lp: LE 6122
mozart piano trio in b flat K502
with erich röhn, violin/arthur troester, cello
unpublished

<u>30 may-6 june 1955/deutsche grammophon sessions
in hamburg thienhaus studio</u>
hansen plays on 1820 hammerklavier (fortepiano)
mozart piano sonatas in c K279 and in e flat K282
lp: LPM 18 320
cd: beulah 2PD 33

<u>9-10 august 1955/deutsche grammophon sessions
in hamburg thienhaus studio</u>
hansen plays on 1820 hammerklavier (fortepiano)
mozart piano sonatas in f K280 and in b flat K281
lp: LPM 18 320
cd: beulah 2PD 33

<u>28 september 1955/deutsche grammophon session
in hamburg thienhaus studio</u>
hansen plays on 1820 hammerklavier (fortepiano)
mozart piano sonata in f K332
lp: LPM 18 321
cd: 479 5516/beulah 1PD 33

<u>november 1955/deutsche grammophon sessions
in hamburg thienhaus studio</u>
hansen plays on 1820 hammerklavier (fortepiano)
mozart piano sonatas in d K331 and in c K545
lp: LPM 18 322
cd: 479 5516/beulah 1PD 33

8-12 december 1955/deutsche grammophon sessions
in hamburg thienhaus studio
hansen plays on 1820 hammerklavier (fortepiano)
mozart piano sonata in c K309
lp: LPM 18 321
cd: beulah 3PD 33

january 1956/deutsche grammophon sessions in
hamburg thienhaus studio
hansen plays on 1820 hammerklavier (fortepiano)
mozart piano sonata in g K283
lp: LPM 18 322
cd: beulah 2PD 33

1957/rias berlin recording in lankwitz siemensvilla
brahms piano quintet in c minor op 34
with amadeus string quartet
cd: audite 21.425

<u>january-february 1958/deutsche grammophon
sessions in hamburg thienhaus studio</u>
**mozart fantasy in c minor K475; rondo in d K485;
piano sonata in f K533/K494**
lp: LPM 18 479
cd: beulah 3PD 33 (sonata only)
mozart piano sonata in c minor K457
lp: LPM 18 479
cd: beulah 1PD 33
mozart piano sonata in d K284
lp: LPM 18 505
cd: 479 5516/beulah 1PD 33
mozart piano sonata in a minor K310
lp: LPM 18 505 cd: beulah 1PD 33

<u>1 june 1959/norddeutscher rundfunk recording
in hamburg</u>
brahms piano quartet in c minor op 60
with erich röhn, violin/erich doberitz. viola/
arthur troester, cello
cd: musicaphon M 56845

<u>1959/sessions for bertelsmann schallplattenring</u>
schubert trout quintet D667
with strub string quartet
lp: bertelsmann 13353
franz schmidt piano quintet in g
with strub string quartet
unpublished

<u>undated eurodisc sessions in bamberg kulturraum</u>
beethoven piano concerto no 1 in c op 15
with bamberger symphoniker/heinz wallberg
lp: KK 70796/KK 70797/opera 3959

<u>undated sessions for europäischer phonoklub
in bamberg kulturraum</u>
**beethoven piano concerto no 3 in c minor
op 37**
with bamberger symphoniker/istvan kertesz
lp: 3269/parnass S 61425

<u>23-25 september 1964/columbia sessions in berlin-dahlem evangelisches gemeindehaus</u>
beethoven clarinet trio in b flat op 11;
brahms clarinet trio in c minor op 115
with heinrich geuser, clarinet/arthur troester, cello
lp: C 80902/SMC 80902/mace MCS 9088

<u>1982-1983/digital recordings for the signal label</u>
mozart piano sonata in c K545; alla turca
from sonata K331; rondo in d K485;
fantasy in d minor K397

<u>1982-1983/performances recorded in lippstadt for a documentary entitled "rückblick auf zehn jahrzehnte" (ein film von rotraut arnold)</u>
schubert impromptu D899 no 3; brahms
ballade op 118 no 3; mozart fantasy
in c minor K475

LUDWIG HOELSCHER cellist 1907-1996

<u>1935-1936/grammophon sessions in berlin</u>
<u>lützowstrasse studio</u>
schubert piano trio in b flat D898
with elly ney. piano/max strub, violin
425	57045/decca X 157
383	
387	57046/decca X 158
426	
385	57047/decca X 159
386	
388	57048/decca X 160
389	

dvorak piano trio in e minor op 90 "dumky"
with elly ney, piano/max strub, violin
482	15107/decca LY 6109
483	
484	15108/decca LY 6110
485	
486	15109/decca LY 6111
487	
488	15110/decca LY 6112
489	

schubert arpeggione sonata in a D821
with elly ney, piano
2RA 566	EH 920/victor (japan) JH 22
2RA 567	
2RA 568	EH 921/victor (japan) JH 23
2RA 569	

cd: classical record ARC 39

1935-1936/electrola sessions/concluded

reger prelude and gavotte from cello suite in d minor

2RA 1223   EH 966
2RA 1224

boccherini rondo for cello and piano; gluck reigen seliger geister arranged for cello and piano

with elly ney, piano

OD 1978   EG 3041
OD 1979

1936/electrola sessions in berlin

with max strub, violin/jost raba, second violin/ walter trampler, viola (strub quartet)

reger string quartet in e flat: 1st & 2nd movements

2RA 1274   EH 971
2RA 1275
2RA 1276   EH 972
2RA 1277

third & fourth movements were recorded in 1938 and the entire work then renumbered as EH 1264-1267

schubert string quartet in g D887

2RA 1706   EH 1039
2RA 1707
2RA 1708   EH 1040
2RA 1709
2RA 1710   EH 1041
2RA 1711
2RA 1712   EH 1042
2RA 1713
2RA 1714   EH 1043
2RA 1715

1936/electrola sessions/concluded
karl hoeller scherzo from string quartet op 24
ORA 3016   EG 6423
ORA 3017

1937-1938/electrola sessions in berlin
pfitzner duo for violin, cello and orchestra
with max strub, violin/staatskapelle berlin/
hans pfitzner
2RA 2633   DB 4508
2RA 2634
2RA 2635   DB 4509
2RA 2636
lp: E 60802/WDLP 703
cd: emi 555 2252/preiser 90029

beethoven piano trio in d op 71 "geister"; third movement from piano trio in d op 9 no 2
with elly ney, piano/max strub, violin
2RA 2678   DB 4587
2RA 2679
2RA 2680   DB 4588
2RA 2681
2RA 2682   DB 4589
2RA 2683
2RA 2684   DB 4590
2RA 2031
lp: E 60564
cd: hänssler 94 047 (op 71)/94 048 (op 9 no 2)

1937-1938/electrola sessions in berlin/concluded
pfitzner cello sonata op 1
with ludwig funk, piano
2RA 2798   DB 4629
2RA 2799
2RA 2796   DB 4630
2RA 2797
2RA 2800   DB 4631
2RA 2801

16 may 1938/electrola sessions in berlin
schubert trout quintet D667; scherzo from piano trio D929
with elly ney, piano/max strub, violin/walter trampler, viola/heinz schubert, double-bass
2RA 2936   DB 4533
2RA 2937
2RA 2938   DB 4534
2RA 2939
2RA 2940   DB 4535
2RA 2941
2RA 2942   DB 4536
2RA 2943
2RA 2944   DB 4537
2RA 2945
lp: E 80838

1938/electrola sessions in berlin
reger string quartet in e flat: 3rd & 4th movements
with max strub, violin/jost raba, second violin/
walter trampler, viola (strub quartet)

2RA 3012	EH 1205
2RA 3013	
2RA 3014	EH 1206
2RA 3015	

schumann cello concerto in a minor op 129
with staatskapelle berlin/joseph keilberth

2RA 3027	DB 4550
2RA 3028	
2RA 3029	DB 4551
2RA 3030	
2RA 3031	DB 4552
2RA 3032	

1939/grammophon sessions in berlin
alte-jakob-strasse studios
schumann piano quartet in e flat; haydn
rondo all'ungarese from piano trio no 25
with elly ney, piano/florizel von reuter, violin/
walter trampler, viola

492	15087/decca CA 8213
493	
494	15088/decca CA 8214
495	
496	15089/decca CA 8215
497	
498	15090/decca CA 8216
499	

cd: hänssler 94 048

52

<u>1939/grammophon sessions in berlin/concluded</u>
brahms piano trio in b op 8
with elly ney, piano/wilhelm stross, violin

716	27316
717	
718	27317
719	
720	27318
721	
722	27319

cd: classical record ACR 39

<u>16 february 1939/reichsrunndfunk recording
in berlin haus des rundfunks</u>
pfitzner cello concerto no 2 op 42
with orchester des reichssenders berlin/
hans pfitzner

51451	unpublished
51452	
51453	unpublished
51454	
51455	unpublished
51456	

rrg tape number 6107

<u>17 and 25 march 1943/reichsrundfunk recordings in berlin haus des rundfunks</u>
**dvorak rondo in g minor for cello and piano;
valentini suite in c for cello and piano**
with ferdinand leitner, piano
cd: meloclassic MC 3002
beethoven opening movements from the cello sonatas op 5 nos 1 and 2
with elly ney, piano
unpublished

<u>30 october 1944/reichsrundfunk recordings in berlin haus des rundfunks</u>
bach courante and sarabande from cello suite no 3 BWV1009 & sarabande from cello suite no 6 BWV1012
cd: meloclassic MC 3002

<u>24 november 1944/reichsrundfunk recordings in berlin haus des rundfunks</u>
grieg cello sonata; chopin allegro moderato and largo from cello sonata
with michael raucheisen, piano
cd: meloclassic MC 3002

<u>22 november 1947/hessischer rundfunk concert recordings in wiesbaden staatstheater</u>
**brahms piano trio in c minor op 101;
schubert piano trio D898**
with walter gieseking, piano/gerhard taschner, violin
cd: bayer 200 031/dante HPC 128

19 may 1948/deutsche grammophon sessions in munich deutsches museum
arrangements for cello and piano of works by frescobaldi, vitali, vivaldi and wolf
with hans richter-haaser, piano
599
600
601
602

september-november 1948/hessischer rundfunk recordings in frankfurt-am-main
beethoven variations on a theme from handel's judas maccabaeus;   fortner cello sonata
with walter gieseking. piano
cd: bayer 200 032
gieseking sonatina for piano and cello
with walter gieseking, piano
cd: bayer 200 032
ravel piano trio
with walter gieseking, piano/gerhard taschner, violin
cd: bayer 200 032

<u>18 october 1949/sender freies berlin recording in dahlem evangelisches gemeindehaus</u>
karl hoeller cello concerto
with philharmonisches orchester berlin/
wilhelm furtwängler
lp: cetra FE 31
cd: originals SH 834/french furtwängler society SWF 001-002

<u>9-10 may 1953/deutsche grammophon sessions in hannover beethovensaal</u>
grieg cello sonata
with hans richter-haaser, piano
lp: LP 16 097
cd: 479 5516

<u>15-19 december 1953/deutsche grammophon sessions in hannover beethovensaal</u>
richard strauss cello sonata in e; brahms cello sonata in e minor op 38
with hans richter-haaser, piano
lp: LPM 18 178
cd: 479 5516

<u>14 june 1955/bayerischer rundfunk recordings in munich</u>
beethoven cello sonatas in a op 69 and in d op 102 no 2
with elly ney, piano
cd: bayer 200 035

<u>28-31 january 1957/deutsche grammophon sessions in berlin jesus-christus-kirche</u>
boccherini cello concerto in b flat; saint-saens cello concerto no 1 in a minor
with philharmonisches orchester berlin/
otto von matzerath
lp: LPEM 19 089

<u>11-12 february 1957/telefunken sessions in berlin lichterfelde festsäle</u>
valentini cello sonata in e; gluck regen seliger geister; schubert-cassado allegretto grazioso; saint-saens le cygne; ravel piece en forme de habanera
with hans altmann, piano
lp: TW 30127
cd: membran 234 337
bach sarabandes from the six solo cello suites
lp: TW 30125/BLE 43071 (nos. 4-6 only)
cd: membran 234 337

4 october 1957/telefunken sessions in munich
herkulessaal
mendelssohn cello sonata in b flat op 45; chopin cello sonata in g minor
with hans altmann, piano
lp: BLE 14116
cd: membran 234 337
234 337 also includes unpublished stereo version of the chopin sonata

november 1957/telefunken sessions in berlin
lichterfelde festsäle
with elly ney, piano
beethoven cello sonatas in f and in g minor op 5 nos 1 and 2
lp: BLE 14081
cd: membran 234 337
beethoven cello sonatas in a op 69 and in c op 102 no 1; variations on mozart's bei männern
lp: BLE 14087
cd: membran 234 337
beethoven cello sonata in d op 102 no 2; variations on mozart's ein mädchen and handel's judas maccabaeus
lp: BLE 14097
cd: membran 234 337

1957-1958/telefunken sessions in berlin
lichterfelde festsäle
chopin introduction et polonaise brillante; faure après un reve; respighi adagio con variazioni
with michael raucheisen, piano
lp: TW 30042/BLE 43071 (respighi)
cd: membran 234 337
dvorak waldesruhe for cello and piano; rondo in g minor; gaillard sarabande in e; couperin les cherubins; frescobaldi toccata in d
with michael raucheisen, piano
lp: TW 30050/BLE 43071 (all except waldesruhe)
cd: membran 234 337
chopin introduction et polonaise brillante; debussy cello sonata no 1
with hans altmann, piano
lp: TW 30111/BLE 43071 (chopin)/STE 10056
cd: membran 234 337
234 337 includes both mono and stereo versions of the debussy sonata

17-19 june 1958/deutsche grammophon sessions in hannover beethovensaal
brahms cello sonatas in e minor op 38 and in f op 99
with joerg demus, piano
lp: LPM 18 523/SLPM 138 012

23-25 october 1958/telefunken sessions in hamburg osterstrasse studios
dvorak cello concerto in b minor op 104
with philharmonisches staatsorchester hamburg/
joseph keilberth
lp: LT 43009/SLT 43009/LT 6629/STE 10359
cd: warner 9029 56892/membran 234 337

27-29 april 1959/electrola sessions in bielefeld rudolf-oetker-halle
haydn cello concerto in d
with nordwestdeutsche philharmonie/
georg ludwig jochum
lp: SMVP 8017

24-27 august 1961/private concert recordings in stadthalle tutzing
mozart piano quartets K478 and K493;
piano trio K564
with elly ney, piano/wilhelm stross, violin (piano quartets)/heinz endres, violin (piano trio)/
ingo sinnhoffer, viola
cd: arthaus
part of a set with dvd and book entitled
"mondscheinsonate: volspianistin elly ney"

28 april 1964/bayerischer rundfunk recording in munich
beethoven cello sonata in c op 102 no 1
with elly ney, piano
cd: bayer 200 035

GEORG KULENKAMPFF violinist 1898-1948

<u>1926/grammophon sessions</u>
with hermann hoppe, piano
reger prelude from suite in a minor;
ries la capricciosa
231   95018
232
cd: podium legenda POL 1021 (ries)/
POL 1024 (reger)
kreisler allegretto in the style of boccherini
            90017
cd: podium legenda POL 1020

10 january 1928/grammophon sessions
with franz rupp, piano
cyril scott prelude "la danse"; ries la capricciosa
368   95073/27704
369
cd: podium legenda POL 1021 (scott)/
POL 1024 (ries)
tartini fugue from violin sonata no 1;
schubert ave maria
370   95075/brunswick 90332
371
cd: podium legenda POL 1021 (schubert)/
POL 1031 (tartini)
dvorak humoresque no 7; mozart
adagio in e K271
374   67156/brunswick 90269
375
cd: podium legenda POL 1021
mozart work also on decca 78rpm X 211

20 august 1929/ultraphon session
with wolfgang rose, piano
gluck reigen seliger geister; d'ambrosio
canzonetta
10079   B 131/BP 301
10080
cd: podium legenda POL 1021

<u>1931/ultraphon sessions</u>
with orchestra/selmar meyrowitz
corelli la follia
30096   F 137
30097
cd: podium legenda POL 1020
dvorak Indian lament; wieniawski mazurka
10133   B 153
10134
cd: podium legenda POL 1020
adam cantique de noel; gruber stille nacht
            B 148
cd: podium legenda POL 1021

6-8 june 1932/telefunken sessions in berlin
singakademie
with philharmonisches orchester berlin/
paul kletzki
bach adagio from violin concerto BWV1042
18451   F 1193/F 22450
18452
lp: HT 6/648 013
cd: pearl GEMMCD 9946/podium
legenda POL 1034
beethoven violin romance no 2 op 50
18453   F 1142/F 22349
18454
lp: HT 6/648 013/KT 11008
cd: pearl GEMMCD 9946/podium
legenda POL 1021

23 january 1933/telefunken sessions in berlin
with wolfgang rose, piano
kreisler tambourin chinois; poldini poupee valsante;
tchaikovsky neapolitan dance from the seasons
18888   unpublished
18890   unpublished
18891   unpublished

20-22 june 1933/telefunken sessions in berlin singakademie

bruch second movement from violin concerto no 1
with philharmonisches orchester berlin/
paul van kempen
19182   E 1492
19183
lp: masters of the bow MB 1015
cd: podium legenda POL 1034

brahms second movement from the violin concerto
with philharmonisches orchester berlin/
paul van kempen
19184   E 1423/TF 161/FP 1198
19185
lp: masters of the bow MB 1015
cd: podium legenda POL 1027

poldini poupee valsante; tchaikovsky neapolitan dance from the seasons
with franz rupp, piano
19188   A 1535/A 2251
19190
lp: masters of the bow MB 1015
cd: podium legenda POL 1020

albeniz tango from the espana suite; kreisler tambourin chinois
with franz rupp, piano
19189   B 1319
19191
cd: podium legenda POL 1020

7 march 1934/grammophon sessions
with franz rupp, piano
brahms hungarian dance; coiuperin tic-toc choc
907
908
cd: podium legenda POL 1020
wagner albumblatt; debussy menuet from petite suite
479   15095
491

october 1934-february 1935/telefunken sessions
with franz rupp, piano
mozart deutscher tanz; francois schubert
l'abeille; gossec tambourin
20175   A 1794
20176
cd: podium legenda POL 1020 (gossec)/
POL 1021 (mozart and schubert)
paradies sicilienne; desplanes intrada
20177   A 1730
20178
cd: podium legenda POL 1020

2 march 1935/grammophon session
with franz rupp, piano
smetana moderato; brahms hungarian dances nos 5 and 7
5921   62749
5922
cd: podium legenda POL 1021 (smetana and brahms no 7)/POL 1020 (brahms no 5)

3-4 april 1935/telefunken sessions in berlin singakademie
mendelssohn violin concerto in e minor op 64; bach air from the third orchestral suite
with philharmonisches orchester berlin/
hans schmidt-isserstedt
20741   E 1824
20742
20743   E 1825
20744
20745   E 1826
20746
20747   E 1827
20748
lp: artisco C440 0016-0017
cd: podium legenda POL 1022 (mendelssohn)/ POL 1021 (bach)

15 april 1935/telefunken sessions in berlin
singakademie
spohr violin concerto no 8 "gesangsszene";
schumann abendlied
with philharmonisches orchester berlin/
hans schmidt-isserstedt

20772   E 1847
20773
20774   E 1848
20775
20776   E 1849
20777

lp: melodiya M10 42819-42820 (spojr)/
masters of the bow MB 1015
cd: alta nova AN 1 (spohr)/podium legenda
POL 1023 (spohr)/POL 1053 (schumann)

24-29 may 1935/grammophon sessions in berlin
lützowstrasse studio
with wilhelm kempff, piano
beethoven violin sonata in a op 47 "kreutzer"
505   35017/67062/decca CA 8207
506
507   35018/67063/decca CA 8208
508
509   35019/67064/decca CA 8209
518
519   35020/67065/decca CA 8210
520
lp: LPE 17 153/2548 712
cd: 453 8042/andante/podium legenda POL 1031

25-28 june 1936/telefunken sessions in berlin
singakademie
with philharmonisches orchester berlin/
hans schmidt-isserstedt
beethoven violin concerto in d op 61; mozart adagio in e K261 for violin and orchestra

21284	E 2016/G 70004/F 22550/TE 496
21285	
21286	E 2017/G 70005/F 22551/TE 497
21287	
21288	E 2018/G 70006/F 22552/TE 498
21289	
21290	E 2019/G 70007/F 22553/TE 499
21291	
21292	E 2020/G 70008/F 22554/TE 500
21293	
21294	E 2021/G 70009/F 22555/TE 501
21295	

lp: LE 6507/LGX 66017/HT 6/KT 11008/
capitol P 8099 (beethoven)
cd: dutton CDEA 5018/podium legenda
POL 1034 (beethoven)/POL 1014 (mozart)

kulenkampff

<u>21-30 june 1937/telefunken sessions in berlin singakademie</u>
with philharmonisches orchester berlin/
hans schmidt-isserstedt
brahms violin concerto in d op 77; reger andante from violin sonata in a minor
21389   E 2074/TE 528/F 27556
21390
21391   E 2075/TE 529/F 27557
21392
21393   E 2076/TE 530/F 27558
21394
21395   E 2077/TE 531/F 27559
21396
21397   E 2078/TE 532/F 27560
21604
lp: artisco C440 90016-90017/past masters PM 24
cd: pearl GEMMCD 9466/podium legenda POL 1027

<u>20 november 1937/reichsrundfunk concert recording in berlin deutsches opernhaus</u>
with philharmonisches orchester berlin/
karl böhm
schumann violin concerto in d minor op posth
cd: podium legenda POL 1053
this was the actual world premiere performance

<u>20 and 31 december 1937/telefunken sessions in berlin singakademie</u>
with philharmonisches orchester berlin/
hans schmidt-isserstedt

schumann violin concerto in d minor op posth: bach gavotte and rondo from solo partita BWV1006

22686	E 2395/TE 655
22687	
22688	E 2396/TE 656
22689	
22690	E 2397/TE 657
22691	
22692	E 1298/TE 658
22726	

lp: HT 5/648 013/melodiya M10 42819-42820
cd: 843 765/4509 936722/dutton CDBP 5018/
podium legenda POL 1020 (bach)/POL 1022

22 june 1938/telefunken sessions in berlin
with ferdinand leitner, piano
ravel menuet; ibert jeux
23261   A 2653
23265
cd: podium legenda POL 1020
lully gavotte from les ballets du roy;
svendsen romance in g
23264   A 2625/T 66
23266
lp: masters of the bow MB 1015
cd: 3984 269192 (svendsen)/podium legenda POL 1020

28 march-6 april 1939/telefunken sessions in berlin singakademie
with orchester der städtischen oper/arthur rother
mozart violin concerto in a K219
24137   E 3044
24138
24139   E 3045
24140
24141   E 3046
24142
24143   E 3047
24144
lp: HT 5/KT 11008/642 216
tchaikovsky violin concerto in d op 35
24158   E 3010/F 18094
24159
24160   E 3011/F 18095
24161
24162   E 3012/F 18096
24163
24164   E 3013/F 18097
24165
lp: LE 6512/HT 26/GMA 101
beethoven violin romance op 40
24168   E 2904
24169
lp: HT 6
cd: podium legenda POL 1021

29 september 1939/grammophon session in berlin
lützowstrasse studio
with franz rupp, piano
schubert ave maria; mozart adagio in e K261
1259   67204
1260
cd: podium legenda POL 1021

21 april 1940/telefunken sessions in berlin
with siegfried schulze, piano
beethoven violin sonata in a op 47 "kreutzer"
          E 3108
          E 3109
          E 3110
          E 3111
lp: HT 15
cd: podium legenda POL 1031

4 june 1940/avro concert recording in
amsterdam concertgebouw
with concertgebouworkest/eduard van beinum
rudi stephan musik für geige und orchester
cd: q-disc 97015/podium legenda POL 1025
podium legenda incorrectly dated 1944

15 june 1940/telefunken sessions In berlin
singakademie
beethoven violin sonata in f op 24 "spring"
with siegfried schulze, piano
25024   E 3124
25025
25026   E 3125
25027
25028   E 3125
25029
lp: HT 15
cd: podium legenda POL 1032

19-25 june 1941/telefunken sessions in berlin
singakademie

grieg violin sonata no 3 in c minor
with siegfried schulze, piano
25911   E 3284
25912
25913   E 3285
25914
25915   E 3286
25916
cd: podium legenda POL 1025

franck violin sonata in a
with siegfried schulze, piano
25917   E 3268
25918
25919   E 3269
25920
25921   E 3270
25922
25023   E 3271
25924
cd: podium legenda POL 1025

<u>19-25 june 1941/telefunken sessions/concluded</u>
dvorak violin concerto in a minor op 53
with philharmonisches orchester berlin/
eugen jochum
25925   SK 3237/G 18033
25926
25927   SK 3238/G 18034
25928
25929   SK 3239/G 18035
25930
25931   SK 3240/G 18036
25932
lp: LSK 7004/LGX 66020/HT 26/GMA 101/
capitol P 8052
cd: 9031 704432/podium legenda POL 1028
bruch violin concerto no 1 in g minor op 26
with philharmonisches orchester berlin/
joseph keilberth
25933   SK 3172
25934
25935   SK 3173
25939
25938   SK 3174
cd: 9031 704432/alta nova AN 1/profil medien
PH 18019/podium legenda POL 1023

kulenkampff

<u>7-8 february 1944/reichsrundfunk concert recording
in berlin philharmonie</u>
sibelius violin concerto in d minor op 47
with philhamonisches orchester berlin/
wilhelm furtwängler
lp: melodiya M10 45909 004/nippon columbia
DXM 112/french furtwängler society SWF 8604/
unicorn UNI 107/eternal 825 764
cd: melodiya MEL 10 00718/russian compact
disc RCD 25009/music and arts CD 799/
archipel ARPCD 0014/chibas restorations 1125/
berliner philharmoniker BPHR 180 181/
podium legenda

<u>1943/reichsrundfunk recording in berlin
haus des rundfunks</u>
mozart violin concerto no 7 K271
with grosses rundfunk-sinfonie-orcheser/
arthur rother
cd: podium legenda POL 1014

16 january 1944/avro concert recording in amsterdam concertgebouw
max reger violin concerto in d minor
with concertgebouworkest/willem van otterloo
cd: podium legenda POL 1024

10 february 1944/danish radio recording in copenhagen
dvorak violin concerto in a minor op 35
with danish state radio orchestra/
svend christian felumb
unpublished

2 february 1946/swiss radio (beromünster) recording in studio bern
richard flury violin concerto no 3
with stadtorchester bern/karl rothenbühler
cd: podium legenda POL 1014

<u>25 june 1946/swiss radio (beromünster)
recordings in studio bern</u>
with willi girsberger, piano
tartini violin sonata in g minor "didone abbandonata"; pizetti aria in d; ibert jeux; debussy nocturne; hubay zephyr; ysaye reve d'enfant; sarasate introduction and tarantelle; paganini caprices op 1 nos 13, 20 and 24
cd: podium legenda POL 1019

<u>1946/swiss radio (beromünster) recording in studio bern</u>
with willi girsberger, piano
beethoven violin sonata in a op 47 "kreutzer"
cd: podium legenda POL 1019
first movement missing from the recording

23-28 january 1947/decca sessions in zürich radio studio

bruch violin concerto no 1 in g minor op 26
with tonhalle-orchester/carl schuricht
ARS 70   AK 1603/LA 223
ARS 71
ARS 72   AK 1604/LA 223
ARS 73
ARS 74   AK 1605/LA 223
ARS 75
lp: artisco C440 0016-0017
cd: 483 1643

23-28 january 1947/decca sessions/concluded
with georg solti, piano
brahms violin sonata in g op 78
ARS 76   AK 1705/K 23013
ARS 77
ARS 78   AK 1706/K 23014
ARS 79
ARS 80   AK 1707/K 23015
ARS 81
lp: CM 9506/ACL 250/ECM 823/
KD 11020/R 23213
cd: podium legenda POL 1045
brahms violin sonata in a op 100
SAR 346   K 2083/T 5304
SAR 347
SAR 348   K 2084/T 5305
SAR 349
SAR 350   K 2085/T 5306
SAR 351
lp: CM 9506/ACL 250/ECM 832/
KD 11020/R 23213
cd: urania URN 22 112/podium
legenda POL 1045

<u>8 july 1947/decca sessions in geneva radio studios</u>
brahms double concerto in a minor op 102
with enrico mainardi, cello/orchestre de la
suisse romande/carl schuricht
SAR 274   AK 2025/LA 147
SAR 275
SAR 276   AK 2026/LA 147
SAR 277
SAR 278   AK 2027/LA 147
SAR 279
SAR 280   AK 2028/LA 147
SAR 281
cd: 483 1643/podium legenda POL 1028

<u>30 march 1948/swedish radio recording
in stockholm</u>
glazunov violin concerto in a minor
with swedish radio orchestra/tor mann
cd: alta nova AN 1/podium legenda POL 1023

july 1948/decca sessions in zürich radio studio
with georg solti, piano
beethoven violin sonata in a minor op 47 "kreutzer"

        K 28119

        K 28120

        K 28121

        K 28122

lp: CM 9507/ACL 211/ECM 831/
KD 11020/R 23214
cd: urania URN 22 112/podium legenda POL 1032

mozart violin sonata in b flat K454
SAR 352   K 2101/EDA 108
SAR 353
SAR 354   K 2102/EDA 108
SAR 355
SAR 356   K 2103/EDA 108
SAR 357
lp: CM 9507/ACL 211/ECM 831/KD 11020/R 23214

brahms violin sonata in d minor op 108
SAR 362   K 2112
SAR 363
SAR 364   K 2113
SAR 365
SAR 366   K 2114
SAR 367
lp: CM 9506/ACL 250/EDM 832/KD 11020/R 23213
cd: urania URN 22 112/podium legenda POL 1045

ENRICO MAINARDI cellist 1897-1976

<u>11 october 1933/grammophon sessions in berlin</u>
<u>hochschule für musik</u>
strauss don quixote op 35
with staatskapelle berlin/karl reitz, viola/
richard strauss
724   35007/brunswick 90319/decca LY 6087
725
726   35008/brunswick 90320/decca LY 6088
727
728   35009/brunswick 90321/decca LY 6089
729
730   35010/brunswick 90322/decca LY 6090
731
732   35011/brunswick 90323/decca LY 6091
lp: 2740 160
cd: 429 9252/479 2703/dutton CDBP 9746/
membran 232 597/doremi DHR 7926-7928

<u>1934/reichssender frankfurt recording</u>
pizzetti cello concerto
with frankfurter funkorchester/hans rosbaud
unpublished

<u>1934/reichssender breslau recording</u>
boccherini cello concerto in b flat
with breslauer funkorchester/ernst prade
unpublished

1941/avro concert recording in amsterdam
concertgebouw
malipiero cello concerto
with concertgebouworkest/eduard van beinum
cd: q-disc 97017/doremi DHR 7926-7928

28 january 1941/grammophon sessions in berlin
alte-jakob-strasse studios
valentini minuet; old robin grey (folksong)
with aldo schoen, piano
8794   unpublished
8797
pergolesi aria; saint-saens le cygne
with michael raucheisen, piano
8795   unpublished
8796

14 october 1941/grammophon sessions in berlin
alte-jakob-strasse studios
with dresdener philharmonie/paul van kempen
dvorak cello concerto in b minor op 104
1649   LM 67 893
1650
1651   LM 67 894
1652
1653   LM 67 895
1654
1655   LM 67 896
1656
1657   LM 67 897
1658

16 december 1941/grammophon session in
berlin alte-jakob-strasse studios
with sebastian peschko, piano
vivaldi largo; bach toccata BWV564
1765   LM 67 883/LM 68 159
1766

january-june 1942/grammophon sessions in berlin
alte-jakob-strasse studios
schumann cello concerto in a minor
with staatskapelle berlin/paul van kempen
1917   LM 67 943
1918
1919   LM 67 944
1920
1921   LM 67 945
1922
chopin cello sonata in g minor
with sergio lorenzi, piano
2231   LM 68 092
2232
2233   LM 68 093
2234
2235   LM 68 094
2236
2237   LM 68 095

december 1942-february 1943/grammophon
sessions in berlin alte-jakob-strasse studios
with sergio lorenzi, piano
chopin nocturne in c sharp minor op posth;
breval rondo from sonata in g
2179   LM 68 091
2180
cd: meloclassic MC 3013 (chopin)
schumann abendlied
2238   LM 68 138
weber sonatina in a
          LM 68 287
cd: meloclassic MC 3013
according to meloclassic these were reichsrundfunk recordings in haus des rundfunks

8 july 1947/decca sessions in geneva radio studios
brahms double concerto in a minor op 102
with georg kulenkampff, violin/orchestre
de la suisse romande/carl schuricht
SAR 274   AK 2025/LA 147
SAR 275
SAR 276   AK 2026/LA 147
SAR 277
SAR 278   AK 2027/LA 147
SAR 279
SAR 280   AK 2028/LA 147
SAR 281
cd: 483 1643/podium legenda POL 1028

28 september-2 october 1948/decca sessions in london west hampstead studios
bach cello suite no 1 BWV1007
AR 12743   AX 434
AR 12748
AR 12744   AX 435
AR 12747
AR 12745   AX 436
AR 12746
bach cello suite no 2 BWV1008
AR 12757   AK 2155/LA 131
AR 12762
AR 12758   AK 2156/LA 131
AR 12761
AR 12759   AK 2157/LA 131
AR 12760

24 august 1949/swiss radio concert recording in lucerne kunsthaus
brahms double concerto in a minor op 102
with wolfgang schneiderhan, violin/
schweizerisches festspielorchester/
wilhelm furtwängler
lp: japan W 19
cd: as-disc AS 372/music and arts CD 1018/
urania URN 22 114/Japanese furtwängler centre WFHC 003

<u>11 october 1949/berliner rundfunk recording
in haus des rundfunks</u>
dvorak cello concerto in b minor op 104
with rundfunk-sinfonie-orchester berlin/
arthur rother
cd: meloclassic MC 3013

<u>19 november 1949/radio bremen concert recording
in grosser glockensaal</u>
with philharmonisches staatsorchester/
hellmut schnackenburg
schumann cello concerto in a minor op 129
cd: meloclassic MC 3013

<u>20-23 january 1950/decca sessions in london
west hampstead studios</u>
bach cello suite no 3 BWV1009
lp: LX 3069/LL 403 (usa)
bach cello suite no 4 BWV1010
lp: LXT 2673/LL 404 (usa)

<u>8-9 october 1950/deutsche grammophon
sessions in munich deutsches museum</u>
schubert arpeggione sonata D
with guido alberto borciani, piano
2161   LVM 72 041
2162
2163   LVM 72 042
2164
lp: LP 16 043/LPE 17 157/
cd: forgotten records FR 457

5 november 1950/süddeutscher rundfunk concert
recording in stuttgart-degerloch
haydn cello concerto in d
with orchester des süddeutschen rundfunks/
carl schuricht
cd: hänssler SWR 93150

27 september 1951 and 20 june 1952/deutsche
grammophon sessions in berlin jesus-christus-kirche
haydn cello concerto in c
with philharmonisches orchester berlin/
fritz lehmann
3977   LVM 72 127
3978
3979   LVM 72 128
3980
lp: LP 16 023/LPE 17 188/LPM 18 222/89 770/
eterna 820 292/decca (usa) DL 7536
cd: 479 5516/forgotten records FR 182

2 december 1951/bayerischer rundfunk
recording in munich
with wolfgang schneiderhan, violin/
edwin fischer, piano
brahms piano trio in c op 87
lp: discocorp BWS 739
cd: music and arts CD 739/deutsche
grammophon 431 3472/431 3432

1952/rca italiana recordings
with carlo zecchi, piano
brahms cello sonatas nos 1 and 2
lp: rca italiana ML 20170
cd: doremi DHR 7926-7928
chopin cello sonata; debussy cello sonata;
schumann adagio and allegro op 70;
vivaldi cello sonata in a
lp: rca italiana ML 20205
boccherini two cello sonatas;
marcello cello sonata in f
lp: rca italiana ML 20224
cd: doremi DHR 7926-7928

1-2 july and 1 september 1952/deutsche grammophon sessions in berlin esplanadesaal
chopin nocturne in c sharp minor; gluck reigen seliger geister; paradis sicilienne; schubert ave maria; grazioli adagio in g minor; schumann abendlied
with michael raucheisen, piano
    LV 36 110 (schubert)
45: NL 32 103 (schubert and schumann)/ EPL 30 455 (gluck, grazioli and schumann)
lp: LPEM 19 054
cd: forgotten records FR 457 (grazioli, schubert and schumann)

9 august 1952/sender rot-weiss-rot concert recordings
in grosser saal des salzburger mozarteums
with wolfgang schneiderhan, violin/
edwin fischer, piano
mozart piano trio in c K548
lp: discocorp BWS 735
cd: music and arts CD 840
beethoven piano trio in b flat op 97 "archduke"
lp: discocorp BWS 735/cetra LO 518
cd: orfeo C593 021
brahms piano trio in c op 87
unpublished

8 august 1953/sender rot-weiss-rot concert recordings
in grosser saal des salzburger mozarteums
with wolfgang schneiderhan, violin/
edwin fischer, piano
schumann piano trio in d minor op 63
lp: cetra DOC 35/discocorp BWS 735
cd: arkadia CDHP 568
beethoven piano trio in d op 70 no 1 "ghost"
lp: cetra DOC 35/discocorp BWS 735
cd: arkadia CDHP 568/orfeo C593 021
brahms piano trio in b op 8
lp: cetra DOC 35

30 november 1953/bayerischer rundfunk recording in munich
with edwin fischer, piano/wolfgang schneiderhan/violin
brahms piano trio in b op 8
lp discocorp BWS 739
cd: music and arts CD 739/amadeo 431 3472/431 3432

20 december 1953/rai concert recordings in rome
with edwin fischer, piano/wolfgang schneiderhan, violin
brahms piano trios in a op 8 and in c op 87
unpublished

5-6 april 1954/deutsche grammophon sessions in hannover beethovensaal
with günther weissenborn, piano
schumann fünf stücke im volkston
lp: LPEM 19 054

12-13 april 1954/deutsche grammophon archiv sessions in hannover beethovensaal
bach cello suites no 1 BWV1007 and no 2 BWV1008
lp: APM 14 029
cd: tower records PROA 59

<u>4 august 1954/oesterreichischer rundfunk concert recordings in salzburg mozarteum</u>
with edwin fischer, piano/wolfgang schneiderhan, violin
brahms the 3 piano trios: in b op 8, in c op 87 and in c minor op 101
lp: cetra DOC 55
cd: arkadia CDHP 568

<u>august 1954/rehearsal recording in lucerne kunsthaus</u>
with edwin fischer, piano/wolfgang schneiderhan, violin
schubert piano trio in b flat D929
unpublished

<u>29 october and 19-20 november 1954/deutsche grammophon archiv sessions in hannover beethovensaal</u>
bach cello suites no 3 BWV1009 and no 4 BWV1010
lp: APM 14 044
cd: tower records PROA 59

<u>24-26 november 1954/deutsche grammophon sessions in berlin jesus-christus-kirche</u>
with rias-sinfonie-orchester/fritz lehmann
schumann cello concerto in a minor
lp: LPE 17 192/LPM 18 222/89 770/
eterna 820 292
cd: 479 5516/forgotten records FR 182

7 december 1954/hessischer rundfunk concert
recording in frankfurt-am-main
with sinfonieorchester des hessischen rundfunks/
karl böhm
haydn cello concerto in d
cd: green hill GH 0003/memories MR 2042

24-31 january 1955/deutsche grammophon sessions
in berlin jesus-christus-kirche
with philharmonisches orchester berlin/
fritz lehmann
dvorak cello concerto in b minor op 102
lp: LPM 18 236/478 442/89 520
cd: forgotten records FR 226/pristine audio PASC 308

23-25 february 1955/deutsche grammophon
archiv sessions in hannover beethovensaal
bach cello suite no 5 BWV1011
lp: AP 13 034
cd: tower records PROA 59

27-30 may 1955/deutsche grammophon sessions
in hannover beethovensaal
with carlo zecchi, piano
**beethoven cello sonata in a op 69; variations
on mozart's bei männern**
lp: LPM 18 353
cd: tower records PROA 141

<u>17-20 october 1955/deutsche grammophon
sessions in hannover beethovensaal</u>
with carlo zecchi, piano
beethoven cello sonatas op 5
no 1 in f and no 2 in g
lp: LPM 18 352
cd: tower records PROA 141
beethoven cello sonatas op 102
no 1 in f and no 2 in d
lp: LPM 18 354
cd: tower records PROA 141

<u>24-28 october 1955/deutsche grammophon archiv
sessions in hannover beethovensaal</u>
bach cello suite no 6 BWV1012
lp: APM 14 061
cd: tower records PROA 59

<u>17 march 1956/hessischer rundfunk recording
in frankfurt-am-main</u>
with carlo zecchi, piano
beethoven cello sonata in c op 102 no 1
cd: meloclassic MC 3000

<u>3 april 1956/hessischer rundfunk recordings
in frankfurt-am-main</u>
with carlo zecchi, piano
brahms cello sonata in e minor op 38;
bach cello sonata BWV1028
cd: meloclassic MC 3000/orfeo C418 971 (bach)

12 august 1956/oesterreichischer rundfunk
concert recording in salzburg festspielhaus
with wiener philharmoniker/karl böhm/
wolfgang schneiderhan, violin
brahms double concerto in a minor
cd: disques refrain DR 92 0039/orfeo C359 941/
datum 12305

15 february 1957/bayerischer rundfunk concert
recording in munich herkulessaal
with sinfonieorchester des bayerischen rundfunks/
eugen jochum
hindemith cello concerto
cd: orfeo C272 931

17-21 june 1957/deutsche grammophon
archiv sessions in munich herkulessaal
with münchner kammerorchester
**haydn cello concerto in d; wagenseil
cello concerto in a**
lp: APM 14 090
cd: forgotten records FR 457
mainardi directs from the cello

31 july 1957/oesterreichischer rundfunk
concert recording in salzburg mozarteum
bach cello suites 1-3 BWV1007-1009
cd: orfeo C360 941

1958/rai torino recording
with orchestra della rai di torino/carlo zecchi
hindemith cello concerto
lp: rococo
cd: doremi DHR 7926-7928

24-29 november 1958/deutsche grammophon
archiv sessions in lucerne neumünster
with lucerne festival strings/rudolf baumgartner
tartini cello concerto in d minor
lp: APM 14 115/SAP 195 001
cd: forgotten records FR 457
vivaldi cello concerto in g RV413
45: EPA 37 185/SEPA 181 005
lp: 89 777
cd: forgotten records FR 457

13 august 1959/oesterreichischer rundfunk
concert recording in salzburg mozarteum
with carlo zecchi, piano
beethoven cello sonata 102 no 1; schubert arpeggione sonata; brahms cello sonata op 38
cd: orfeo C822 101

18 may 1962/rai torino concert recording
in sala del conservatorio
with orchestra sinfonica della rai di torino/
carlo maria giulini
pizzetti cello concerto
lp: rococo
cd: doremi DHR 7926-7928

19-21 january 1963/ariola eurodisc sessions
in berlin meistersaal
bach cello suite no 3 BWV1009
lp: KK 70224/KK 70225/71521-3-5
cd: denon COCO 80165-80167
bach cello suite no 2 BWV1008
lp: KK 70222/KK 70223/71521-3-5
cd: denon COCO 80165-80167

3 march 1963/ariola eurodisc session
in berlin meistersaal
bach cello suite no 1 BWV 1007
lp: KK 70222/KK 70223/71521-3-5
cd: denon COCO 80165-80167

10 may 1963/ariola eurodisc session
in berlin meistersaal
bach cello suite no 4 BWV1010
lp: KK 70224/KK 70225/71521-3-5
cd: denon COCO 80165-80167

1964/hungarian radio recording in budapest
with carlo zecchi, piano
beethoven cello sonatas nos 1 and 2
lp: hungaraton SLPX 31281

<u>22-24 april 1964/ariola eurodisc sessions in berlin meistersaal</u>
bach cello suites no 5 BWV1011 and no 6 BWV1012
lp: KK 71520/KK 71521/71521-3-5
cd: denon COCO 80165-80167

<u>1964-1965/amadeo sessions in vienna</u>
with kammerorchester der wiener staatsoper
boccherini cello concerto in b flat
lp: AVRS 6100/bertelsmann 13133
cd: mace 9077
boccherini largo for cello and orchestra
lp: AVRS 6100/AVRS 15089/bertelsmann 13133
cd: mace 9077
vivaldi cello concerto in c; geminiani concerto grosso op 3 no 2
lp: AVRS 6100/AVRS 15023/bertelsmann 13133
cd: mace 9077
mainardi directs from the cello

<u>3-4 december 1966/private lp recording</u>
with ludwig kaufmann, piano
marcello sonata in f
lp: 629 906

<u>2 march 1973/oesterreichischer rundfunk recording in salzburg landesstudio</u>
with carl seemann, piano
reger cello sonata in a minor op 116
cd: orfeo C418 971

CARL SEEMANN pianist 1910-1983

3 february 1949/deutsche grammophon sessions in hamburg musikhalle
haydn piano sonata no 49 in e flat
1046   LM 68 409
1047
cd: 445 4792
mozart variations on lison dormait K264
             LM 68 406
cd: 477 5856

15-18 september 1950/deutsche grammophon sessions in munich deutsches museum
with münchner philharmoniker/fritz lehmann
mozart piano concerto in c K503
2166   LVM 72 035
2167
2168   LVM 72 036
2169
lp: LP 16 014/479 011/89 799/
decca (usa) DL 9569

15-16 february 1951/deutsche grammophon sessions in hannover beethovensaal
stravinsky serenade in a
2561   LVM 72 071
2563
45: NL 32 214
mozart variations on a theme of gluck K455
lp: LPM 18 308
cd: 445 4792/477 5856

15-16 may 1951/deutsche grammophon sessions
in hannover beethovensaal
beethoven six bagatelles op 126
LVM 72 145
cd: 445 4792
beethoven variations in f minor op 34
LVM 72 144

3-4 february 1952/deutsche grammophon sessions
in hannover beethovensaal
bartok for children
lp: LP 16 041/LPM 18 492
debussy childrens corner
45: NL 32 215
lp: LPM 18 492
cd: 445 4792
mozart piano sonata in c K330
LVM 72 201
lp: LPM 18 218
cd: 477 5856
mozart fantasy in d minor K397
LVM 72 205
45: EPL 30 032
lp: LP 16 113/LPM 18 556-18 557
cd: 477 5856
mozart minuet in f K355
lp: LP 16 113/LPE 17 005
cd: 477 5856
mozart rondo in d K485
lp: LP 16 050/LP 16 113/
LPM 18 556-18 557
cd: 477 5856

5-6 april 1952/deutsche grammophon sessions
in hannover beethovensaal
bartok improvisations on hungarian
peasant songs
lp: LP 16 041/LPM 18 492
bartok sonata for 2 pianos and percussion
with edith picht-axenfeld. second piano/
ludwig porth and karl peinkofer, percussion
3707   LVM 72 215
3708
lp: LP 16 041/LPM 18 384

29 april 1952/deutsche grammophon session
in hannover beethovensaal
brahms ballade op 10 no 1
45: EPL 30 032

23 may 1952/süddeutscher rundfunk
recording in stuttgart
beethoven six bagatelles op 126
cd: orfeo C474 971

3 august 1952/deutsche grammophon
sessions in hannover beethovensaal
brahms fantasien op 116; klavierstücke op 118
lp: LP 16 040 (op 116)/LPM 18 369
cd: 445 4792

28-29 october 1952/deutsche grammophon
sessions in bamberg kulturraum
with bamberger symphoniker/fritz lehmann
mozart rondo for piano and orchestra K382
        LV 36 064
lp: LPM 18 143/478 078/89 716/
decca (usa) DL 4079/DL 9631
cd: 445 4792/474 6112
mozart rondo for piano and orchestra K386
4264   LV 36 075
4265
45: NL 32 210
lp: decca (usa) DL 4079
cd: 474 6112

<u>4-9 december 1952/deutsche grammophon
sessions in hannover beethovensaal</u>

**mozart piano sonatas in a minor K310
and in a K331**
lp: LPM 18 140/LPM 18 556-18 557 (K331)
cd: 445 4792 (K310)/477 5856

mozart piano sonata in c K545
45: NL 32 234
lp: LPM 18 308
cd: 477 5856

**mozart piano sonatas in d K311 and
in d K576**
lp: LP 16 111/LPM 18 508
cd: 477 5856

mozart piano sonata in b flat K570
        LVM 72 288
lp: LPM 18 282
cd: 477 5856

13-17 march 1953/deutsche grammophon
sessions in hannover beethovensaal
mozart adagio K540
lp: LPM 18 308
cd: 477 5856
mozart piano sonatas in c K309 and in b flat K333
lp: LPM 18 150
cd: 477 5856
mozart piano sonatas in b flat K281 and in g K283; minuet in g K1
lp: LP 16 120
cd: 477 5856
mozart piano sonata in c minor K457; fantasy in c minor K475; rondo in a minor K511
lp: LPM 18 251
cd: 477 5856

3-5 june 1953/deutsche grammophon sessions in berlin jesus-christus-kirche
with philharmonisches orchester berlin/ fritz lehmann
mozart piano concerto in d K537 "coronation"
5080   LVM 72 426
5081
5082   LVM 72 427
5083
5084   LVM 72 428
lp: LPM 18 143/478 078/89 716/
decca (usa) DL 9631
cd: 445 4792/474 6112

19-27 september 1953/deutsche grammophon sessions in vienna konzerthaus
with wolfgang schneiderhan, violin
schubert violin sonatinas in d D384 and in g D408
lp: LP 16 085/LPM 18 502
mozart violin sonata in g K379
lp: LPM 18 260
mozart violin sonatas in e minor K304 and in e flat K380
lp: LP 16 092/LPM 18 323/decca (usa) DL 9886 (K304)/DL 9862 (K380)
mozart violin sonatas in b flat K454 and in a K526
lp: LPM 18 250/LPM 18 556-18 557 (K526)/ decca (usa) DL 9862

20-26 may 1954/deutsche grammophon sessions
in hannover beethovensaal

mozart piano sonata in c K279
lp: LPM 18 298
cd: 477 5856

mozart piano sonata in f K280
lp: LPM 18 282
cd: 477 5856

mozart piano sonata in e flat K282
lp: LPM 18 218
cd: 477 5856

mozart piano sonatas in d K284 and in f K533/K494
lp: LPM 18 205
cd: 477 5856

mozart piano sonata in f K332
lp: LPM 18 200
cd: 477 5856

mozart variations on vous dirai-je mamam K265
lp: LPM 18 290
cd: 477 5856

<u>16-18 december 1954/deutsche grammophon
sessions in hannover beethovensaal</u>
with wolfgang schneiderhan, violin
**schubert violin sonatina in a D385 and
duo in a D574**
lp: LPM 18 241
mozart violin sonata in c K296
lp: LPM 18 307
mozart violin sonata in f K376
lp: LPM 18 316
mozart violin sonata in b flat K378
lp: LPM 18 260

<u>18-20 april 1955/deutsche grammophon
sessions in berlin jesus-christus-kirche</u>
with philharmonisches orchester berlin/
fritz lehmann/andor foldes, second piano
mozart concerto for 2 pianos K365
lp: LP 16 125/LPE 17 240/
479 005/2535 744
cd: 474 6112

13-15 june 1955/deutsche grammophon sessions
in hannover beethovensaal

mozart fantasy in c minor K396
lp: LPM 18 290
cd: 477 5856

mozart variations on lison dormait K264
and on an original theme KA 137
lp: LPM 18 298
cd: 477 5856

allegro in g minor K312
lp: LPM 18 290
cd: 477 5856

mozart variations on a theme by duport K573
lp: LPM 18 282
cd: 477 5856

mozart gigue in g K574
lp: LPM 18 308
cd: 477 5856

<u>6-9 october 1955/deutsche grammophon
sessions in vienna konzerthaus</u>
with wolfgang schneiderhan, violin
**mozart violin sonatas in g K301 and
in e flat K381**
lp: LPM 18 323 /decca (usa) DL 9886
mozart violin sonata in a K305
lp: LPM 18 316
mozart violin sonata in f K377
lp: LPM 18 250/decca (usa) DL 9862
mozart violin sonata in e flat K481
lp: LPM 18 307

<u>18 december 1955/deutsche grammophon
session in hannover beethovensaal</u>
with wolfgang schneiderhan, violin
schumann violin sonata
45: EPL 30 206
lp: LPM 18 502
cd: 445 4792

<u>9-11 december 1956/deutsche grammophon
sessions in hannover beethovensaal</u>
with annelies kupper. soprano
karl amadeus hartmann lamento
lp: LP 16 135/LPE 17 245

6-9 april 1957/deutsche grammophon sessions in
vienna brahmssaal des musikvereins
with wolfgang schneiderhan, violin
bartok violin sonata no 2; hindemith violin sonata no 3; stravinsky duo concertant
lp: LPM 18 400/decca (usa) DL 9980

9-11 may 1957/deutsche grammophon sessions
in berlin jesus-chrisus-kirche
with philharmonisches orchester berlin/
thomas scherman
stravinsky concerto for piano and winds
lp: LPM 18 384

november 1957/deutsche grammophon sessions
in hannover beethovensaal
with wolfgang schneiderhan, violin
brahms violin sonatas nos 1 and 3
lp: LPM 18 696/SLPM 138 696
cd: 463 6532

12-13 november 1957/deutsche grammophon
sessions in hamburg musikhalle
with sinfonieorchester des norddeutschen
rundfunks/hans schmidt-isserstedt
fortner movements for piano and orchestra
lp: LPM 18 405

24-25 november 1957/deutsche grammophon
sessions in munich bavaria film studios
with fritz ortner, bass/bernhard minetti, speaker/
edith picht-axenfeld, harpsichord/rudolf albert
giselher klebe römische elegien
lp: LPM 18 406

4-5 december 1957/deutsche grammophon
sessions in berlin jesus-christus-kirche
with philharmonisches orchester berlin/
ferdinand leitner
mozart piano concerto in c minor K491
lp: LPE 17 183/89 799
cd: 445 4792

14-19 july 1958/deutsche grammophon
sessions in hannover beethovensaal
**bach chromatic fantasy and fugue in d minor;
partita no 1 in b flat; toccata and fugue in d;
sechs kleine präludien**
45: EPL 30 305 (sechs kleine präludien)
lp: LPM 18 322/SLPM 138 017
cd: 445 4792 (chromatic fantasy and fugue)
**brahms waltzes op 39; haydn piano sonatas
no 31 in e and no 38 in e flat; variations
in f minor**
lp: LPEM 19 162/SLPEM 136 021

<u>11-28 may 1959/deutsche grammophon sessions
in vienna brahmssaal des musikvereins</u>
with wolfgang schneiderhan, violin
**beethoven violin sonatas in f op 24 "spring"
and in a op 47 "kreutzer"**
lp: LPM 18 620/SLPM 138 620/
135 148/2535 321
cd: 445 4792 (op 47)
**beethoven violin sonatas in d op 12 no 1,
in a op 12 no 2 and in g op 30 no 3**
lp: LPM 18 621/SLPM 138 621
**beethoven violin sonatas in e flat op 12 no 3,
in a minor op 23 and in a op 30 no 1**
lp: LPM 18 622/SLPM 138 622
**beethoven violin sonatas in c minor
op 30 no 2 and in g op 96**
lp: LPM 18 623/SLPM 138 623

<u>8 october 1959/bayerischer rundfunk recording
in munich herkulessaal</u>
with members of sinfonieorchester des
bayerischen rundfunks/paul hindemith/
wolfgang marschner, violin
berg chamber concerto
cd: orfeo C197 891

16 february 1960/deutsche grammophon sessions
in hannover beethovensaal
with wolfgang schneiderhan, violin
brahms violin sonata no 2; fae scherzo;
franck violin sonata in a
lp: LPM 18 633/SLPM 138 633/
2535 751 (brahms)
cd: 463 6532 (brahms)

10 february 1961/deutsche grammophon
session in berlin
with wolfgang schneiderhan, violin
prokofiev violin sonata op 94
lp: LPM 18 794/SLPM 138 794
cd: 445 4792

9 may 1962/norddeutscher rundfunk
recording in hamburg
beethoven piano sonata in e op 14 no 1
cd: orfeo C474 971

10-11 march 1963/norddeutscher rundfunk
concert recording in hamburg musikhalle
with sinfonieorchester des norddeutschen
rundfunks/istvan kertesz
beethoven piano concerto no 2
in b flat op 19
cd: orfeo C474 971

15 june 1964/süddeutscher rundfunk concert
recording from the schwetzingen festival
with wolfgang schneiderhan, violin
**bach sonata BWV1015; beethoven violin sonata
op 12 no 3; schubert duo D574; mozart
violin sonata K454**
cd: orfeo C473 971

5-6 july 1965/radio bremen recordings
bach the six solo partitas BWV825-830
cd: orfeo C014 002

25 february 1972/norddeutscher rundfunk
concert recording in kiel
with sinfonieorchester des norddeutschen
rundfunks/leopold hager
mozart piano concerto in e flat K449
cd: orfeo C447 961

2 march 1973/oesterreichischer rundfunk
recording in salzburg landesstudio
with enrico mainardi, cello
reger cello sonata in a minor op 116
cd: orfeo C418 971

<u>12-14 november 1979/teldec sessions in berlin teldec studio</u>
mozart fantasy K397; rondo K511; variations K455; clementi piano sonata op 36 no 2; capriccio in f
lp: 642 580

<u>6 december 1979/norddeutscher rundfunk concert recording in hamburg musikhalle</u>
with sinfonieorchester des norddeutschen rundfunks/wilfried boettcher
mozart piano concerto in c K503
cd: orfeo C447 961

MAX STRUB violinist 1900-1966

<u>1935-1936/grammophon sessions in berlin
lützowstrasse studio</u>
with elly ney, piano/ludwig hoelscher, cello
schubert piano trio in b flat   D898
425	57045/decca X 157
383	
387	57046/decca X 158
426	
385	57047/decca X 159
386	
388	57048/decca X 160
389	

dvorak piano trio in e minor op 90 "dumky"
482	15107/decca LY 6109
483	
484	15108/decca LY 6110
485	
486	15109/decca LY 6111
487	
488	15110/decca LY 6112
489	

1936/electrola sessions in berlin

reger string quartet in e flat: 1st & 2nd movements

with jost raba, second violin/walter trampler, viola/ ludwig hoelscher, cello (strub quartet)

2RA 1274   EH 971
2RA 1275
2RA 1276   EH 972
2RA 1277

third and fourth movements of the quartet were recorded in 1938 and the entire work re-numbered as EH 1264-1267 (see page 127)

reger lyrisches andante; burleske from suite no 4; minuet from suite no 5

with elly ney, piano

2RA 1319   EH 969
2RA 1320

cd: classical record ACR 39

schubert string quartet in g D887

with jost raba, second violin/walter trampler, viola/ ludwig hoelscher, cello (strub quartet)

2RA 1706   EH 1039
2RA 1707
2RA 1708   EH 1040
2RA 1709
2RA 1710   EH 1041
2RA 1711
2RA 1712   EH 1042
2RA 1713
2RA 1714   EH 1043
2RA 1715

<u>1937/electrola sessions in berlin</u>
with luther, flute/mazurot, second violin/
hans schrader, cello/ernst kruttge, harpsichord
franz benda presto from violin concerto in a
OD 1705   EG 2869/B 8119
OD 1707
mozart minuet from concerto in d K107; handel andante from trio in c minor
OD 1708   EG 2881
OD 1709

with jost raba, second violin/walter trampler, viola/
ludwig hoelscher, cello (strub quartet)
karl hoeller scherzo from string quartet op 24
ORA 3016   EG 6423
ORA 3017

unidentified works by schubert, schumann,
spohr and corelli may also have been
recorded in these sessions

1937-1938/electrola sessions in berlin
pfitzner duo for violin, cello and orchestra
with staatskapelle berlin/hans pfitzner/
ludwig hoelscher, cello
2RA 2633   DB 4508
2RA 2634
2RA 2635   DB 4509
2RA 2636
lp: E 60802/WDLP 703
cd: emi 555 2252/preiser 90029
beethoven piano trio in d op 70 "geister";
scherzo from piano trio in d op 9 no 2
with elly ney, piano/ludwig hoelscher, cello
2RA 2678   DB 4587
2RA 2679
2RA 2680   DB 4588
2RA 2681
2RA 2682   DB 4589
2RA 2683
2RA 2684   DB 4590
2RA 2031
lp: E 60564
cd: hänssler 94 048 (scherzo)

1937-1938/electrola sessions in berlin/concluded
schubert piano quintet D667 "the trout";
scherzo from piano trio D929
with elly ney, piano/walter trampler, viola/
ludwig hoelscher, cello/heinz schubert, double-bass
2RA 2936   DB 4533
2RA 2937
2RA 2938   DB 4534
2RA 2939
2RA 2940   DB 4535
2RA 2941
2RA 2942   DB 4536
2RA 2943
2RA 2944   DB 4537
2RA 2945
lp: E 80838
reger string quartet in e flat: 3rd & 4th movements
with jost raba, second violin/walter trampler, viola/
ludwig hoelscher, cello (strub quartet)
2RA 3012   EH 1205
2RA 3013
2RA 3014   EH 1206
2RA 3015
first and second movements of the quartet
were recorded in 1936 and the entire work
re-numbered as EH 1264-1267 (see page 124)

1939/electrola sessions in berlin
bach violin concerto in a minor BWV1041
with collegiums musicum berlin/fritz stein
2RA 4088   DB 5527
2RA 4089
2RA 4090   DB 5528
2RA 4091

29-30 june 1939/electrola sessions in dresden semperoper
beethoven violin concerto in d op 61
with sächsische staatskapelle dresden/
karl böhm
2RA 4130   DB 5516
2RA 4131
2RA 4132   DB 5517
2RA 4133
2RA 4134   DB 5518
2RA 4135
2RA 4136   DB 5519
2RA 4137
2RA 4138   DB 5520
2RA 4139
lp: emi 1C137 53500-53504M
cd: toshiba SGR 1201-1204/
warner 9029 588672

1940/electrola sessions in berlin
bruckner string quintet in f
with hermann hubl, second violin/hermann hirschfelder, viola/emil seiler, second viola/ hans münch-holland, cello

2RA 4188	DB 5541
2RA 4189	
2RA 4190	DB 5542
2RA 4191	
2RA 4192	DB 5543
2RA 4193	
2RA 4194	DB 5544
2RA 4195	
2RA 4196	DB 5545
2RA 4197	

cd: pristine audio PACM 0006

1941/electrola sessions in berlin
beethoven string quartet in c op 59 no 3
with hermann hubl, second violin/hermann hirschfelder, viola/hans münch-holland, cello (strub quartet)

2RA 4754	DB 5599
2RA 4755	
2RA 4756	DB 5600
2RA 4757	
2RA 4758	DB 5601
2RA 4759	
2RA 4760	DB 5602
2RA 4761	

6 april 1941/reichsrundfunk recording in leipzig senderaum

schubert string quintet in c D956
with hermann hubl, second violin/hermann hirschfelder, viola/hans münch-holland, cello/ hans schrader, second cello
cd: meloclassic MC 4002

22 march 1943/grammophon sessions in berlin alte-jakob-strasse studios

haydn piano trio in f HOB/XV37
with adrian aeschbacher, piano/
gaspar cassado, cello
2300   LM 68 383
2301
2302   LM 68 384
2304

23 june 1943/reichsrundfunk recording in berlin haus des rundfunks

gerhart von westerman string quartet op 8 no 2
with hermann hubl, second violin/hermann hirschfelder, viola/hans münch-holland, cello
(strub quartet)
cd: meloclassic MC 4002

<u>5 april 1944/reichsrundfunk recordings in hamburg sendesaal</u>
with adrian aeschbacher, piano/gaspar cassado, cello
brahms piano trio in c op 87; mozart andante and allegretto from piano trio in g K564
cd: meloclassic MC 3001

<u>1959/sessions for bertelsmann schallplattenring</u>
schubert piano quintet D667 "the trout"
lp: 13353
franz schmidt piano quintet in g; dvorak finale from string quartet in f op 96 "american"; haydn variations from kaiserquartett

GERHARD TASCHNER violinist 1922-1976

25 november 1941/odeon session in berlin
bach chaconne from solo partita no 2 BWV1004
XXB 8893   O-8764
XXB 8894
XXB 8895   O-8765
XXB 8896
cd: archiphon ARC 128-129/tahra TAH 342

11 march 1942/odeon session in berlin
with grete nette-rothe, piano
paganini violin sonata in e minor; sarasate romanza andaluza from danzas espanolas
XXB 8919   O-8766
XXB 8920
cd: archiphon ARC 128-129/tahra TAH 342

23-26 november 1943/odeon sessions in berlin
with cor de groot, piano
franck violin sonata in a
XXB 9124   O-8793
XXB 9125
XXB 9126   O-8794
XXB 9127
XXB 9128   O-8795
XXB 9129
XXB 9130   O-8796
XXB 9131
cd: archiphon ARC 128-129
handel violin sonata in d HWV371
XXB 9132   O-8797
XXB 9133
XXB 9134   O-8798
XXB 9135
cd: archiphon ARC 128-129/tahra TAH 342

26 november 1942/reichsrundfunk concert
recording in berlin philharmonie
with philharmonisches orchester berlin/
lovro von matacic
dvorak violin concerto in a minor op 53
cd: tahra TAH 641

26-27 october 1944/odeon sessions in berlin
sarasate malaguena; zapateado; zigeunerweisen
XXB 9471
XXB 9472
XXB 9473
XXB 9474
cd: archiphon ARC 128-129
78rpm versions, including alternative takes,
remained unpublished

7-8 november 1944/odeon sessions in berlin
with philharmonisches orchester berlin/
fritz lehmann
bruch violin concerto no 1 in g minor
XXB 9481
XXB 9482
XXB 9483
XXB 9484
XXB 9485
XXB 9486
cd: archiphon ARC 128-129
78rpm version, including an alternative take,
remained unpublished

16 december 1944/reichsrundfunk recording in
berlin haus des rundfunks
with philharmonisches orchester berlin/
hermann abendroth
bruch violin concerto no 1 in g minor
cd: tahra TAH 192-193/archiphon ARC 126/
archipel ARPCD 0232

10 april 1947/berliner rundfunk recording
in haus des rundfunks
with walter gieseking, piano
**franck violin sonata in a; brahms violin
sonata in d minor op 108**
cd: tahra TAH 350-351

24 september 1947/berliner rundfunk recording
in haus des rundfunk
with rundfunk-sinfonie-orchester berlin/
arthur rother
khachaturian violin concerto
cd: archiphon ARC 126

22 november 1947/hessischer rundfunk concert
recording in wiesbaden staatstheater
with walter gieseking, piano/
ludwig hoelscher, cello
**brahms piano trio in c minor op 101;
schubert piano trio in b flat D898**
cd: bayer 200 031/dante HPC 128

11-12 april 1948/rias berlin concert recording
in titania palest
with philharmonisches orchester berlin/
arthur rother
tchaikovsky violin concerto in d op 35
lp: royale 1265
cd: archiphon ARC 128-129
*lp edition was published pseudonymously
with the names fritz machalovsky/berlin
symphony orchestra/joseph balzer*

19 april 1948/rias berlin concert recording
in titania palest
with philharmonisches orchester berlin/
leopold ludwig
beethoven violin concerto in d op 61
lp: royale 1307
*published pseudonymously with the names
jan balachowsky/berlin symphony
orchestra/gerd rubahn*

november 1948/hessischer rundfunk
recording in frankfurt-am-main
with walter gieseking, piano/ludwig
hoelscher, cello
ravel piano trio
cd: bayer 200 032

18 december 1949/rias berlin concert recording
in titania palest
with philharmonisches orchester berlin/
wilhelm furtwängler
wolfgang fortner violin concerto
lp: cetra FE 31
cd: mdg 642 11132/german furtwängler society
TMK 12681/as-disc AS 370/audite 21.403

14 december 1951/südwestfunk recording in
baden-baden
with walter gieseking, piano
beethoven violin sonata op 47 "kreutzer"
cd: tahra TAH 409-412/bayer 200 853

24 march 1952/rias berlin recording in berlin-dahlem
evangelisches gemeindehaus
with philharmonisches orchester berlin/
georg solti
beethoven violin concerto in d op 61
cd: mdg 642 11132

31 october 1952/odeon sessions in berlin
kreisler prelude and allegro in the style of
paganini; variations on a theme of corelli
XXB 9593   O-9183
XXB 9594

24 november 1952/odeon session in berlin
kreisler caprice viennois
XXB 9595   O-9184
XXB 9596

12 december 1952/westdeutscher rundfunk
recording in grosser sendesaal des
kölner funkhauses
with sinfonie-orchester des westdeutschen
rundfunks/rudolf kempe
hindemith kammermusik no 4
cd: emi 566 5242

21 august 1953/bayerischer rundfunk concert
recordings in bamberg zentralsaal
with bamberger symphoniker/fritz lehmann
mendelssohn violin concerto in e minor op 64;
sarasate carmen fantasy
cd: emi 566 5242

19 september 1953/westdeutscher rundfunk
recording in grosser sendesaal des
kölner funkhauses
with sinfonie-orchester des westdeutschen
rundfunks/georg ludwig jochum
bruch violin concerto no 1 in g minor
cd: emi 566 5242

<u>1954/bayerischer rundfunk recordings in munich</u>
with hans altmann, piano
schubert violin sonatina D384; paganini caprice in a minor
cd: archipel ARPCD 0232

<u>17 april 1955/rias berlin concert recording in hochschule für musik</u>
with rias-sinfonie-orchester/rudolf kempe
pfitzner violin concerto op 34
cd: archipel ARPCD 0400

<u>28 april 1955/hessischer rundfunk recording in frankfurt-am-main</u>
with sinfonie-orchester des hessischen rundfunks/gustav könig
pfitzner violin concerto op 34
cd: emi 566 5242

8-9 may 1955/norddeutscher rundfunk concert recording in hamburg musikhalle
with sinfonie-orchester des norddeutschen rundfunks/hans schmidt-isserstedt
khachaturian violin concerto
cd: tahra TAH 641

20-21 december 1955/rias berlin recording in villa lankwitz
with rias-sinfonie-orchester/georg ludwig jochum
wolfgang fortner violin concerto
cd: emi 566 5242

1956/westdeutscher rundfunk recording in grosser sendesaal des kölner funkhauses
with sinfonie-orchester des westdeutschen rundfunks/herbert sandberg
sibelius violin concerto
cd: archipel ARPCD 0232

143
FRIEDRICH WUEHRER   pianist 1900-1975

<u>22 september 1937/electrola sessions in berlin</u>
scriabin etude in d sharp minor and
waltz in f minor
ORA 2293   EG 6224
ORA 2294
scriabin nocturnes in f sharp minor and in a
ORA 2295   EG 6297
ORA 2296
reger humoreske in c and gavotte in e
ORA 2297   EG 6122
ORA 2298

<u>June 1939/electrola session in berlin</u>
beethoven rondp op 129 "rage over a lost penny"
ORA 3990   EG 6905
ORA 3991
beethoven polonaise in op 89
ORA 3992   EG 7024
ORA 3993

<u>12 october 1944/reichsrundfunk recording</u>
<u>in vienna musikvereinssaal</u>
with wiener philharmoniker/karl böhm
grieg piano concerto in a minor
lp: urania (usa) URLP 7015/royale 1264
royale edition was published pseudonymously
with the names gerhard stein/berlin
symphony orchestra/karl list

15 october 1944/reichsrundfunk recording in
berlin staatsoper unter den linden
with philharmonisches orchester berlin/
eugen jochum
**franz schmidt variations on a theme
by beethoven**
cd: tahra TAH 382-385

10 november 1944/reichsrundfunk recording
in vienna konzerhaus
with michael raucheisen, second piano
weber sonata for 2 pianos op 39
unpublished

december 1944/reichsrundfunk recordings
in vienna konzerthaus
**chopin etudes op 25; haydn variations
in f minor**
lp: melodiya M10 46829 006
cd: dante HPC 094
beethoven bagatelles in f, a and c
lp: melodiya M10 46829 006
beethoven variations op 76; fantasy op 77
unpublished

12 november 1947/columbia sessions in vienna
brahmssaal des musikvereins
schubert moments musicaux D780
CHAX 342   unpublished
CHAX 343
CHAX 344   unpublished
CHAX 345
CHAX 346   unpublished

15-24 november 1947/columbia sessions in vienna brahmssaal des musikvereins
with hermann von nordberg, second piano/ irmgard seefried, soprano (op 52)/elisabeth höngen, contralto (op 52)/hugo meyer-welfing, tenor (op 52)/hans hotter, bass-baitone (op 52)
brahms liebeslieder-walzer op 52;
waltzes op 39: nos 2, 6 and 15
CHAX 347   LX 1114/LCX 118/LVX 55
CHAX 348
CHAX 349   LX 1115/LCX 119/LVX 56
CHAX 350
CHAX 351   LX 1116/LCX 120/LVX 57
CHAX 352
CHAX 353   LX 1117/LCX 121/LVX 58
CHAX 360
lp: world records SH 373 (op 52)
cd: preiser 90356 (op 52)/emi 566 4252
78rpm edition also issued in automatic coupling with catalogue numbers LX 8628-8631

23 november-11 december1947/columbia sessions
in vienna brahmssaal des musikvereins
with wolfgang schneiderhan, violin
beethoven violin sonata in f op 24 "spring"
CHAX 355   unpublished
CHAX 356
CHAX 357   unpublished
CHAX 358
CHAX 359   unpublished
beethoven violin sonata un c minor op 30 no 2;
schumann allegretto from violin sonata op 105
CHAX 362   LX 1190
CHAX 363
CHAX 364   LX 1191
CHAX 365
CHAX 366   LX 1192
CHAX 373
CHAX 374   LX 1193
CHAX 382
lp: melodiya M10 46983 006
cd: partita PC 9207-9208
78rpm edition also issued in automatic coupling
with catalogue numbers LX 8673-8676
bach largo from violin sonata BWV1017
CHAX 381   unpublished

5-14 november 1949/columbia sessions in vienna
brahmssaal des musikvereins
scriabin piano sonatas nos 3 and 4
CHAX 504   unpublished
CHAX 505
CHAX 506   unpublished
CHAX 507
CHAX 508   unpublished
CHAX 509

1950/vox session in vienna konzerthaus
with wiener symphoniker/wiener akademiechor/
clemens krauss
beethoven choral fantasy op 80
lp: PL 6480/PL 10640
cd: tuxedo TUXCD 9001/archipel ARPCD 0137/
crq editions CRQCD 121/preiser 90553

1950/sender rot-weiss-rot recording in
vienna brahmssaal des musikvereins
with niederoesterreichisches
tonkünstlerorchester/karl randoff
beethoven piano concerto no 4 in g op 58
lp: remington 199-72

31 august-2 september 1950/vox sessions in
vienna symphonia studios
with wiener symphoniker/rudolf moralt
mendelssohn piano concerto no 2 in d minor
lp: PL 6570
cd: crq editions CRQCD 281-282

8-11 january 1952/deutsche grammophon sessions
in vienna konzerthaus
with wolfgang schneiderhan, violin
brahms violin sonata no 1 in g op 78
       LVM 72 175

       LVM 72 176

lp: LP 16 027/LPM 18 295
brahms violin sonata no 2 in a op 100
       LVM 72 181

       LVM 72 182

lp: LPM 18 295/melodiya M10 46989 006
cd: partita PC 9207-9208
brahms violin sonata no 3 in d minor op 108
lp: LPM 18 144

1952-1953/vox schubert piano sonata sessions in vienna konzerthaus
schubert piano sonata in d D575
lp: PL 8420/VBX 9/dover HCR 5207
cd: beurac BRC 2980/diapaison DIAP 08/
crq editions CRQCD 197-198
schubert piano sonata in a minor D784
lp: PL 8210/VBX 9
cd: beurac BRC 2981/crq editions CRQCD 197-198
schubert piano sonata in c minor D958
lp: PL 8420/VBX 9/dover HRC 5207
cd: beurac BRC 2980/crq editions CRQCD 138-139
schubert piano sonata in b flat D960
lp: PL 8210/VBX 9
cd: beurac BRC 2981/crq editions CRQCD 138-139

18-19 april 1952/vox sessions in vienna konzerthaus
with wiener symphoniker/rudolf moralt
dvorak piano concerto in g minor op 33
lp: PL 7630

4-5 july 1952/vox sessions in vienna brahmssaal des musikvereins
with wiener symphoniker/rudolf moralt
anton rubinstein piano concerto no 4
lp: PL 7780

17 november 1952/süddeutscher rundfunk
recording in stuttgart-untertürkheim

**beethoven piano sonata in b flat op 106
"hammerklavier"**

cd: meloclassic MC 1023

1952-1956/vox schubert piano sonata sessions
in vienna konzerthaus

schubert piano sonata in a D557

lp: VBX 11

cd: beurac BRC 2981/diapaison DIAP 08/
crq editions CRQCD 331-332

schubert piano sonata in f minor op 625

lp: PL 9800/VBX 11

cd: beurac BRC 2981/crq editions CRQCD 217-218

schubert piano sonata in c D840

lp: VBX 11

cd: beurac BRC 2981/crq editions CRQCD 138-139
(movements 1 and 2)/CRQCD 197-198
(movements 3 and 4)

*this unfinished sonata is recorded in the completion
(movements 3 and 4) by ernst krenek*

<u>1952-1953/vox schubert piano sonata sessions in vienna konzerthaus/concluded</u>

schubert piano sonata in d D850
lp: PL 8820/VBX 10
cd: beurac BRC 2981/crq editions CRQCD 197-198

schubert piano sonata in g D894
lp: PL 8590/VBX 10
cd: beurac BRC 2980/crq editions CRQCD 197-198

<u>1953-1954/vox sessions in vienna konzerthaus</u>

grieg piano concerto in a minor
with wiener symphoniker/heinrich hollreiser
lp: PL 9000/VBX 1

beethoven piano concerto no 1 in c op 15; rondo in b flat for piano and orchestra
with wiener symphoniker/hans swarowsky
lp: PL 8400/STPL 513 070
cd: tahra TAH 704-707 (concerto)

brahms piano concerto no 1 in d minor op 15
with wiener symphoniker/hans swarowsky
lp: PL 8000/GBY 12180/orbis BL 704
cd: tahra TAH 704-707/crq editions CRQCD 217-218

beethoven piano concerto no 5 in e flat op 73 "emperor"; variations op 76
with wiener symphoniker/heinrich hollreiser
lp: PL 9490/GBY 11740
cd: tahta TAH 704-707 (concerto)

orchestra described as vienna pro musica for PL 8400 and PL 9490

<u>5 april 1954/süddeutscher rundfunk recordings in stuttgart-untertürkheim</u>
schubert wanderer fantasy D760; beethoven variations on a russian dance WoO71
cd: meloclassic MC 1023

<u>June 1954/vox sessions in vienna</u>
with reinhold barchet, violin/hermann hirschfelder, viola/helmut reimann, cello/heinz unger, cello/ karl krüger, double-bass
schubert trout quintet D667; notturno D897
lp: PL 8970/dover HCR 5206/parnass 70068

<u>7-12 december 1954/vox sessions in vienna konzerthaus</u>
scriabin piano concerto in f sharp minor
with wiener symphoniker/hans swarowsky
lp: PL 9200
orchestra described on this recording as vienna pro musica

<u>december 1954/vox sessions in vienna konzerthaus</u>
with wiener symphoniker/heinrich hollreiser
tchaikovsky piano concerto no 1 in b flat minor op 23
lp: PL 9000
cd: crq editions CRQCD 281-282
tchaikovsky piano concerto no 2 in g op 44
lp: PL 9200
cd: crq editions CRQCD 281-282
orchestra described on these recordings as vienna pro musica

<u>1955-1956/vox schubert piano sonata sessions in vienna konzerthaus</u>

schubert piano sonata in e D459
lp: PL 9800/VBX 11
cd: bearac BRC 2981/diapaison DIAP 08/
crq editions CRQCD 331-332

schubert piano sonata in a minor D537
lp: PL 9130/VBX 10
cd: bearac BRC 2981/crq editions CRQCD 217-218

schubert piano sonata in e minor D566
lp: VBX 11
cd: bearac BRC 2980/crq editions CRQCD 331-332

schubert piano sonata in a minor D845
lp: PL 9620/VBX 9
cd: bearac BRC 2980/crq editions CRQCD 138-139

schubert piano sonata in a D959
lp: PL 9130/VBX 10
cd: bearac BRC 2981/crq editions CRQCD 138-139

<u>june 1955/vox sessions in vienna konzerthaus</u>
brahms piano concerto no 2 in b flat op 83
unpublished

february-march 1956/vox sessions in stuttgart liederhalle
beethoven triple concerto in c op 56
with württembergisches staatsorchester/ walther davisson/bronislav gimpel, piano/ joseph schuster, cello
lp: GBY 11660
cd: tahra TAH 704-707
orchestra described on this recording as stuttgart pro musica

brahms cello sonata op 38; richard strauss cello sonata op 5
with joseph schuster, cello
lp: LP 9910

beethoven the complete cello sonatas and variations for cello and piano
with joseph schuster, cello
lp: VBX 8/SVBX 58

13 april 1956/berliner rundfunk recording in haus des rundfunks
with rundfunk-sinfonie-orchester berlin/ hermann abendroth
schumann piano concerto in a minor op 54
lp: eterna 826 955
cd: berlin classics BC 20522

<u>june 1956/vox schubert piano sonata sessions in vienna konzerthaus</u>

schubert piano sonata in e D157
lp: VBX 11
cd: bearac BRC 2980/diapaison DIAP 08/
crq editions CRQCD 331-332

schubert piano sonata in c D279
lp: PL 9620/VBX 9
cd: bearac BRC 2981/diapaison DIAP 08/
crq editions CRQCD 331-332

schubert piano sonata in e flat D568
lp: PL 8820/VBX 10
cd: bearac BRC 2981/crq editions CRQCD 197-198

schubert piano sonata in a D664
lp: PL 8590/VBX 10
cd: bearac BRC 2981/crq editions CRQCD 217-218

1956-1958/vox sessions in vienna konzerthaus
weber piano concerti nos 1 and 2
with wiener symphoniker/hans swarowsky
lp: PL 8140
orchestra described on this recording as vienna pro musica
liszt paganini etude in e minor; brahms paganini variations; schumann etudes after paganini caprices
lp: PL 8850
cd: crq editions CRQCD 394-395
schumann davidsbündlertänze; piano sonata no 3 (concerto without orchestra)
lp: PL 8860
cd: crq editions CRQCD 217-218 (davidsbündler)/ CRQCD 394-395 (sonata)
beethoven the last 3 piano sonatas opp 109-111
lp: PL 9900
cd: crq editions CRQCD 281-282/ tahra TAH 704-707

12-13 september 1957/vox sessions in bamberg kulturraum
with bamberger symphoniker/jonel perlea
beethoven piano concerto o 4 in g op 58
lp: PL 10640
cd: pristine audio PASC 139/tahra TAH 704-707

december 1957/vox sessions in baden-baden
with sinfonie-orchester des südwestfunks/
michael gielen
prokofiev piano concerto no 2 in g minor
lp: PL 12100
prokofiev piano concero no 3 in d
lp: PL 12190/STPL 513 130
these recordings formed part of a cycle of the complete prokofiev piano concerti which also involved other pianists and conductors

1958-1960/vox sessions in stuttgart liederhalle
with württembergisches staatsorchester/
walther davisson
brahms piano concerto no 2 in b flat op 83
lp: PL 9790
cd: tahra TAH 704-709/crq editions
CRQCD 281-282
**beethoven piano concerti no 2 in b flat op 19
and no 3 in c minor op 37**
lp: PL 9570/STPL 513 060/orbis
CX 20320 (concerto no 3)
cd: tahra TAH 704-707
orchestra described for these recordings as stuttgart pro musica

30 january 1961/ortf recording in paris radio france studios
**schubert piano sonata in a minor D784;
brahms 3 intermezzi op 117; variations
and fugue on a theme by handel**
lp: vogue 672 001
cd: crq editions CRQCD 331-332

INDEX OF REPERTOIRE INCLUDED IN THE DISCOGRAPHIES

numbers refer to pages on which the works occur; many pieces are instrumental arrangements of existing vocal or orchestral compositions

ADOLPHE ADAM (1803-1856)

cantique de noel

63

ISAAC ALBENIZ (1860-1909)

tango from espana suite

65

JOHANN SEBASTIAN BACH (1685-1750)

toccata BWV564

89

toccata and fugue in d minor BWV565

17

solo keyboard partita BWV825

117   120

solo keyboard partita BWV826

120

solo keyboard partita BWV827

120

solo keyboard partita BWV828

120

solo keyboard partita BWV829

120

solo keyboard partita BWV830

120

bach/continued

chromatic fantasy and fugue in d minor BWV903
117
air from third orchestral suite
67
chaconne from solo violin partita BWV1004
133
gavotte & rondeau from solo violin sonata BWV1006
72
solo cello suite BWV1007
56 (sarabande)   91   96
100   102
solo cello suite BWV1008
56 (sarabande)   91   96
100   102
solo cello suite BWV1009
53 (courante and sarabande)   56 (sarabande)
92   97   100   102
solo cello suite BWV1010
56 (sarabande)   92   97
102
solo cello suite BWV1011
56 (sarabande)   98   103
solo cello suite BWV1012
53 (sarabande)   56 (sarabande)
99   103

bach/concluded
keyboard sonata BWV1015
120
cello sonata BWV1028
99
violin concerto in a minor BWV1041
128
adagio from violin concerto BWV1042
64
concerto for three pianos BWV1063
14
concerto for three pianos BWV1064
33
sechs kleine präludien
117

WILHELM FRIEDEMANN BACH (1710-1784)
four polonaises
27

BELA BARTOK (1881-1945)
violin sonata no 2
116
sonata for two pianos and percussion
107
for children
106
improvisations on hungarian peasant songs
107

LUDWIG VAN BEETHOVEN (1770-1827)
piano concerto no 1 in c op 15
14   44   151
piano concerto no 2 in b flat op 19
119   157
piano concerto no 3 in c minor op 37
23   26   29   30
38   44   157
piano concerto no 4 in g op 58
38   147   156
piano concerto no 5 in e flat op 73 "emperor"
31   35   39   151
rondo in b flat for piano and orchestra
151
violin concerto in d op 61
70   128   137   138
violin romance no 1 op 40
74
violin romance no 2 op 50
64
triple concerto in c op 56
154
choral fantasy op 80
147

beethoven/continued

piano sonata in c minor op 10 no 1
39
piano sonata in c minor op 13 "pathetique"
30
piano sonata in e op 14 no 1
119
piano sonata in d minor op 31 no 3 "tempest"
15
piano sonata in e flat op 81a "les adieux"
15
piano sonata in e minor op 90
58
piano sonata in b flat op 106 "hammerklavier"
150
piano sonata in e op 109
156
piano sonata in a op 110
156
piano sonata in c minor op 111
39   156
variations in f minor op 34
106
variations on an original theme op 76
144   151
variations on a russian dance
152
polonaise op 89
143

beethoven/continued

six bagatelles op 126
22 (no 6)   106   107
144 (nos 2. 4 and 5)
ecossaise in e flat
16
fantasy op 77
144
für elise
16
rondo in c op 51 no 1
15
rondo capriccioso op 120
15
rondo op 129 "rage over a lost penny"
143
clarinet trio in b flat op 11
45
violin sonata in d op 12 no 1
118
violin sonata in a op 12 no 2
118
violin sonata in e flat op 12 no 3
118   120

beethoven/continued

violin sonata in a minor op 23
118

violin sonata in f op 24 "spring"
76   118   146

violin sonata in a op 30 no 1
118

violin sonata in c minor op 30 no 2
118   146

violin sonata in g op 30 no 3
118

violin sonata in a op 47 "kreutzer"
69   81   85   75
118   138

violin sonata in g op 96
118

cello sonata in f op 5 no 1
53 (first movement)   57   99
102   154

cello sonata in g minor op 5 no 2
53 (first movement)   57   99
102   154

cello sonata in a op 69
56   57   98   154

cello sonata in c op 102 no 1
57   59   99 (2 versions)
101   154

cello sonata in d op 102 no 2
56   57   99   104
154

beethoven/concluded

variations for cello and piano on a theme by handel (see the conquering hero)
54 57 154

variations for cello and piano on a theme by mozart (bei mannern welche liebe fühlen)
57 98 154

variations for cello and piano on a theme by mozart (ein mädchen oder weibchen)
57 98 154

third movement from piano trio in d op 9 no 2
49 126

piano trio in d op 71 "ghost"
49 95 126

piano trio in b flat op 97 "archduke"
94

string quartet in c op 59 no 3
129

JOHANN GEORG BENDA (1713-1752)
presto from violin concerto in d
125

ALBAN BERG (1885-1935)
chamber concerto
118

167

LUIGI BOCCHERINI (1743-1805)
cello concerto in b flat
56   87   103
largo for cello and orchestra
103
rondo for cello and piano
48
2 cello sonatas
94

JOHANNES BRAHMS (1833-1897)
piano concerto no 1 in d minor op 15
39   151
piano concerto no 2 in b flat op 83
13   16   153   157
violin concerto in d op 77
65 (second movement)   71
double concerto in a minor op 102
84   90   91   100
violin sonata in g op 78
83   94   116   148
violin sonata in a op 100
83   94   119   148
violin sonata in d minor op 108
85   116   136   148
fae scherzo for violin and piano
119

brahms/continued

cello sonata in e minor op 38
55   58   94   99
101   154
cello sonata in f op 99
58   94
piano sonata in f minor op 5
39
ballade op 10 no 1
107
ballade op 118 no 3
45
ballade op 118 no 5
37
fantasien op 116
107
intermezzi op 117 nos 1, 2 and 3
22   157 (no 3)
intermezzo op 117 no 7
37
intermezzo op 119 no 1
39
klavierstücke op 118
107
rhapsodien op 79 nos 1 and 2
15
handel variations
157
paganini variations
156

brahms/concluded

hungarian dances
66   67

walzer op 39
117   145 (nos 2, 6 and 15)

liebeslieder-walzer op 52
145

clarinet trio in e minor op 115
45

piano quartet in c minor op 60
43

piano quintet in c minor op 34
42

piano trio in b op 8
52   95   96 (2 versions)
97

piano trio in c op 87
13   93   95   96
97   131

piano trio in c minor op 101
53   97   136

JEAN BAPTISTE BREVAL (1766-1823)
rondo from sonata in g
90

MAX BRUCH (1838-1920)
violin concerto no 1 in g minor op 26
65 (second movement)   78   82
135   136   139

ANTON BRUCKNER (1824-1896)
string quintet in f
129

WILLIAM BYRD (1543-1623)
will you walk through the woods?
28

FRYDERIK CHOPIN (1810-1849)
etudes op 25
144
introduction et polonaise brillante
58 (2 versions)
nocturne in e flat op 9 no 2
37
nocturne in c sharp minor op posth
90   94
ccllo sonata in g minor
53 (allegro and largo)   56   89
94

MUZIO CLEMENTI (1752-1832)
piano sonata op 36 no 2
121
capriccio in f
121

ARCANGELO CORELLI (1653-1713)
la follia
63

FRANCOIS COUPERIN (1688-1733)
les cherubins
58
le tic-toc-choc
66

ALFREDO D'AMBROSIO (1871-1914)
canzonetta op 6
62

CLAUDE DEBUSSY (1862-1918)
fantaisie pour piano et orchestre
22   25
childrens corner
106
minstrels from preludes book 1
21
ondine from preludes book 2
21
menuet from petite suite
66
nocturne
81
cello sonata no 1
58   94

172
JEAN-ANTOINE DESPLANES (1678-1760)
intrada
66

ANTONIN DVORAK (1841-1904)
piano concerto in g minor op 33
109
violin concerto in a minor op 35
78   80   135
cello concerto in b minor op 104
59   88   92   98
piano trio in e minor op 90 "dumky"
40   47   123
finale from string quartet in f op 96 "american"
131
rondo in g minor for cello and piano
53   58
waldesruhe for cello and piano
58
humoresque op 7
62
indian lament
63

EDUARD ERDMANN (1896-1958)
foxtrot in c
21

GABRIEL FAURE (1845-1924)
apres un reve
58

RICHARD FLURY (1896-1967)
violin concerto no 3
80

WOLFGANG FORTNER (1907-1987)
movements for piano and orchestra
116
violin concerto
138   141
cello sonata
54

CESAR FRANCK (1822-1890)
prelude fugue et chorale
37
violin sonata in a
77   119   134   136

GIROLAMO FRESCOBALDI (1583-1643)
toccata in d
58

JOHANN ERNST GAILLARD (1680-1749)
sarabande in e
58

FRANCESCO GEMINIANI (1687-1782)
concerto grosso op 3 no 2
103

WALTER GIESEKING (1895-1956)
sonatina for cello and piano
54

ALEXANDER GLAZUNOV (1865-1936)
violin concerto in a minor
84
nocturne op 37
21

CHRISTOPH WILLIBALD GLUCK (1714-1787)
reigen seliger geister from orfeo ed euridice
48   56   62   94

FRANCOIS JOSEPH GOSSEC (1734-1829)
tambourin
66

GIOVANNI BATTISTA GRAZIOLI (1746-1820)
adagio in g minor for cello and piano
94

EDVARD GRIEG (1843-1907)
piano concerto in a minor
18   143   151
violin sonata no 3 in c minor
77
cello sonata
53   55

FRANZ XAVER GRUBER (1787-1863)
stille nacht heilige nacht
63

GEORGE FRIDERIC HANDEL (1685-1759)
keyboard suite no 6
26
violin sonata in d
133
andante from trio in c minor
125
chaconne in g
11

KARL AMADEUS HARTMANN (1905-1963)
lamento
115

FRANZ JOSEF HAYDN (1732-1809)
cello concerto in d
59   93   98   100
cello concerto in c
93
piano trio no 25 in g
12   51 (rondo all'ongarese)
piano trio no 37 in f
130
variations from the kaiserquartett
131

haydn/concluded
piano sonata no 31 in e
117
piano sonata no 38 in e flat
117
piano sonata no 49 in e flat
105
variations in f minor
24   117   144

STEPHAN HELLER (1813-1888)
berceuse (prelude no 15)
27

PAUL HINDEMITH (1895-1963)
cello concerto
100   101
kammermusik no 4
139
violin sonata no 3
116

KARL HOELLER (1907-1972)
cello concerto
55
scherzo from string quartet op 24
49   125

177
JENO HUBAY (1868-1937)
zephyr
81

JACQUES IBERT (1890-1962)
jeux
73   81

ARAM KHACHATURIAN (1903-1978)
violin concerto
136   141

GISELHER KLEBE (1925-2009)
römische elegien
117

FRITZ KREISLER (1875-1962)
allegretto in the style of boccherini
61
caprice viennois
139
prelude and allegro in the style of paganini
138
tambourin chinois
64   65
variations on a theme of corelli
138

178

ERNST KRENEK (1900-1991)
kleine suite
21
completion of schubert piano sonata D840
150

FRANZ LISZT (1811-1886)
piano concerto no 1 in e flat
36
paganini etude in e minor
156
mephisto polka
26
valse oubliee no 1
26

JEAN BAPTISTE LULLY (1632-1687)
gavotte from les ballets du roy
73

GIAN FRANCESCO MALIPIERO (1882-1973)
cello concerto
88

BENEDETTO MARCELLO (1686-1739)
cello sonata in f
94   103

179

FELIX MENDELSSOHN-BARTHOLDY (1809-1847)

piano concerto no 2 in d minor

147

violin concerto

67   139

cello sonata in b flat

57

DARIUS MILHAUD (1892-1974)

piano sonata

25

WOLFGANG AMADEUS MOZART (1756-1791)

minuet from piano concerto in d K107

125

piano concerto in e flat K449

120

piano concerto in d minor K466

23

piano concerto in c minor K491

24   117

piano concerto in c K503

105   121

piano concerto in d K537 "coronation"

36   111

concerto for two pianos K365

113

mozart/continued

rondos for piano and orchestra K382 and K386
108
violin concerto no 5 K219
74
violin concerto no 7 K271
62 (adagio)   70 (adagio)   75 (adagio)   79
piano quartets K478 and K493
59
piano trio in b flat K502
40
piano trio in c K548
95
piano trio in g K564
13 (adagio and allegretto)   59
131 (adagio and allegretto)
piano sonata in c K279
41   112
piano sonata in e K280
41   112
piano sonata in b flat K281
41   110
piano sonata in e flat K282
41   112
piano sonata in g K283
37   42   110

mozart/continued

piano sonata in d K284
43   112

piano sonata in c K309
42   110

piano sonata in a minor K310
43   109

piano sonata in d K311
109

piano sonata in c K330
106

piano sonata in d K331
41   45 (alla turca)   109

piano sonata in f K332
41   112

piano sonata in b flat K333
110

piano sonata in c minor K457
43   110

piano sonata in f K533/K594
29   43   112

piano sonata in c K545
41   45   109

piano sonata in b flat K570
109

piano sonata in d K576
109

182

mozart/continued

deutscher tanz
66
adagio K540
110
allegro K312
114
fantasy K396
114
fantasy K397
45   106   121
fantasy K475
43   45   110
gigue K574
114
minuet K1
110
minuet K355
106
rondo K485
37   43   45   106
rondo K511
110   121
variations on an original theme K137
114
variations on lison dormait K264
105   114

mozart/continued

variations on ah vous dirai-je mamam K265
112
variations on a theme by dupont K373
114
variations on a theme by gluck K455
105   131
violin sonata in c K296
113
violin sonata in g K301
115
violin sonata in e minor K304
111
violin sonata in a K305
115
violin sonata in f K376
113
violin sonata in f K377
115
violin sonata in b flat K378
113
violin sonata in g K379
111
violin sonata in e flat K380
111
violin sonata in e flat K381
115

184

mozart/concluded

violin sonata in b flat K454
85   111   120

violin sonata in e flat K481
115

violin sonata in a K526
111

MODEST MUSSORGSKY (1839-1881)

pictures in an exhibition
29   31

NICCOLO PAGANINI (1782-1840)

violin sonata in e minor
133

caprice in a minor
140

three caprices from op 1
81

MARIA THERESIA VON PARADIES (1759-1824)

sicilienne
66   94

GIOVANNI BATTISTA PERGOLESI (1710-1736)

aria
88

HANS PFITZNER (1869-1949)
violin concerto
140 (2 versions)
cello concerto no 2
52
duo for violin, cello and orchestra
49   126
cello sonata op 1
50

ILDEBRANDO PIZETTI (1880-1968)
cello concerto
87   101
aria in d
81

EDUARD POLDONI (1869-1957)
poupee valsante
64   65

SERGE PROKOFIEV (1891-1953)
piano concerti nos 2 and 3
157
violin sonata in d
119

MAURICE RAVEL (1875-1937)
piano trio
54   137
piece en forme de habanera
56
menuet
73

MAX REGER (1873-1916)
piano concerto in f minor
27   28   31
violin concerto in d minor
80
andante from violin sonata in a minor
71
string quartet in e flat
48   51   124   127
cello sonata in a minor
103   120
prelude and gavotte from cello suite in d minor
48
movement from deutsche tänze for 4 hands
39
burleske from suite no 4
104
humoreske and gavotte
143
lyrisches andante
124
minuet from suite no 5
124
prelude from suite in a minor
61

187

OTTORINO RESPIGHI (1879-1936)
adagio con variazioni
58

FRANZ RIES (1755-1846)
la capricciosa
61   62

ANTON RUBINSTEIN (1829-1894)
piano concerto no 4
149

CAMILLE SAINT-SAENS (1835-1921)
cello concerto no 1 in a minor
56
le cygne
56   88

PABLO DE SARASATE (1844-1908)
introduction et tarantelle
81
carmen fantasy
139
malaguena
135
romanza andaluza from danzas espanolas
133
zapateado
135
zigeunerweisen
135

188
FRANZ SCHMIDT (1874-1939)
variations on a theme by beethoven
144
piano quintet in g
44   131

ARNOLD SCHOENBERG (1874-1961)
sechs klavierstücke op 19
25

FRANCOIS SCHUBERT (1808-1878)
l'abeille
66

FRANZ SCHUBERT (1797-1828)
arpeggione sonata
47   92   101
trout quintet D667
12   17   44   50
127   131   152
piano trio in b flat D898
47   53   123   136
piano trio in e flat D929
40   50 (scherzo)   95
127 (scherzo)
notturno D897
40   152
ave maria
62   75   95

schubert/continued

piano sonata in e D157
155
piano sonata in c D279
155
piano sonata in e D459
153
piano sonata in a minor D537
153
piano sonata in D557
150
piano sonata in e minor D566
153
piano sonata in e flat D568
155
piano sonata in d D575
29   149
piano sonata in f minor D625
150
piano sonata in a D664
26 (2 versions)   28   154
piano sonata in a minor D784
149   157
piano sonata in c D840 (completion by krenek)
150
piano sonata in a minor D845
153

schubert/continued

piano sonata in f D850
151

piano sonata in g D894
30   15

piano sonata in c minor D958
27   28   31   149

piano sonata in a D959
25   31   32   153

piano sonata in b flat D960
17   27 (2 versions)   29
30   149

zwölf deutsche tänze D790
24

allegretto D915
30

allegretto grazioso
56

wanderer fantasy D760
17   152

string quartet in d D887
48   124

string quintet in c D956
130

schubert/continued

impromptu in c minor D899 no 1
11   19   30
impromptu in e flat D899 no 2
11   19   30
impromptu in g D899 no 3
11   19   30   45
impromptu in a flat D899 no 4
11   19   30
impromptu in f minor D935 no 1
11   19   31
impromptu in a flat D935 no 2
11   14   19   27
31
impromptu in b flat D935 no 3
11   19   31
impromptu in f minor D935 no 4
11   19   31
moment musical in c D780 no 1
13   17   145
moment musical in a flat D780 no 2
13   17   145
moment musical in f minor D780 no 3
13   17   27   145

schubert/concluded

moment musical in c sharp minor D780 no 4
13   17   145
moment musical in f minor D780 no 5
13   17   145
moment musical in a flat D780 no 6
13   17   145
violin sonatina in d D384
111   140
violin sonatina in d D385
113
violin sonatina in g D408
111
duo in a D574
113   120

ROBERT SCHUMANN (1810-1856)
piano concerto in a minor op 54
154
konzertstück for piano and orchestra op 92
25   29
violin concerto in d minor
71   72
cello concerto in a minor
51   89   92   97
piano sonata no 3 (concerto without orchestra)
156

schumann/continued

violin sonata op 105
115   146 (allegretto)

cello sonata op 5
154

fünf stücke im volkston for cello and piano
96

adagio and allegro for cello and piano
94

piano trio in d minor
95

piano quartet in e flat
51

abendlied
68   90   94

album für die jugend op 68
17

arabeske op 18
19

blumenstück op 19
19

davidsbündlertänze op 6
15   156

etudes after paganini caprices
156

fantasiestücke op 12
28 (2 versions)

schumann/concluded

impromptu on themes of clara wieck
29

intermezzi op 4
27

kinderszenen op 15
18

romanzen op 28
16

toccata op 7
19

waldszenen op 82
19

CYRIL SCOTT (1879-1970)

la danza
62

ALEXANDER SCRIABIN (1872-1916)
piano concerto in f sharp minor
152
piano sonata no 3
147
piano sonata no 4
147
etude in d sharp minor
143
nocturne in f sharp minor
143
nocturne in a
143
waltz in f minor
143

JEAN SIBELIUS (1865-1957)
violin concerto in d minor op 47
79   141

BEDRICH SMETANA (1824-1884)
hochzeitsszenen nos 1 and 2
21
moderato
67

LUDWIG SPOHR (1784-1859)
violin concerto no 8 "gesangsszene"
68

RUDI STEPHAN (1887-1915)
musik für geige und orchester
75

RICHARD STRAUSS (1864-1949)
don quixote
87
cello sonata
55

IGOR STRAVINSKY (1882-1971)
concerto for piano and winds
116
duo concertant
116
serenade in a
105

JOHAN SEVERIN SVENDSEN (1840-1911)
romance in g
73

GIUSEPPE TARTINI (1692-1770)
cello concerto in d minor
101
violin sonata in g minor
62 (fugue)   81

197
PIOTR TCHAIKOVSKY (1840-1893)
piano concerto no 1 in b flat minor op 23
34	40	152
piano concerto no 2 in g minor op 44
152
violin concerto in d op 35
74	137
neapolitan dance from the seasons
64	65

HEINZ TIESSEN (1887-1971)
die amsel
21
ein sperling in die hand des eduard erdmann
21

GIOVANNI VALENTINI (1585-1649)
cello suite in c
53
cello sonata in e
56
minuet 88

ANTONIO VIVALDI (1678-1741)
cello concerto in c
103
cello concerto in g
101
cello sonata in a
94
largo
89

198
GEORG CHRISTOPH WAGENSEIL (1715-1777)
cello concerto in a
100

RICHARD WAGNER (1813-1883)
albumblatt
66

CARL MARIA VON WEBER (1786-1826)
piano concerto no 1
29   31   156
piano concerto no 2
156
sonata for 2 pianos
144
sonatina in c
90

GERHART VON WESTERMANN (1894=1963)
string quartet op 8 no 2
130

HENRI WIENIAWASKI (1835-1880)
mazurka
63

199
EUGENE YSAYE (1858-1931)
reve d'enfant
81

ARRANGEMENTS FOR CELLO AND PIANO OF UNIDENTIFIED WORKS BY FRESCOBALDI, VITALI, VIVALDI AND WOLF
54

OLD ROBIN GREY (FOLKSONG)
88

Books published by Travis & Emery Music Bookshop:

Anon.: Hymnarium Sarisburiense, cum Rubricis et Notis Musicis.
Anon.: Säcularfeier des Geburtstages von Ludwig van Beethoven
Agricola, Johann Friedrich from Tosi: Anleitung zur Singkunst.
Allen, Percy: The Stage Life of Mrs. Stirling: With ... C19th Theatre
Bach, C.P.E.: edited W. Emery: Nekrolog or Obituary Notice of J.S. Bach.
Bateson, Naomi Judith: Alcock of Salisbury
Bathe, William: A Briefe Introduction to the Skill of Song
Berlioz, Hector: Autobiography of Hector Berlioz, (2 vols.)
Buckley, Robert John: Sir Edward Elgar
Burney, Charles: The Present State of Music in France and Italy
Burney, Charles: The Present State of Music in Germany, The Netherlands ...
Burney, Charles: Account of an Infant Musician
Burney, Charles: An Account of the Musical Performances ... Handel
Burney, Karl: Nachricht von Georg Friedrich Handel's Lebensumstanden.
Burns, Robert: The Caledonian Musical Museum .. Best Scotch Songs. (1810)
Cobbett, W.W.: Cobbett's Cyclopedic Survey of Chamber Music. (2 vols.)
Corrette, Michel: Le Maitre de Clavecin
Cox, John Edmund: Musical Recollections of the Last Half Century. (2 vols.)
Crimp, Bryan: Dear Mr. Rosenthal ... Dear Mr. Gaisberg ...
Crimp, Bryan: Solo: The Biography of Solomon
Crotch, William: Substance of Several Courses of Lectures on Music
d'Indy, Vincent: Beethoven: Biographie Critique
d'Indy, Vincent: Beethoven: A Critical Biography
d'Indy, Vincent: Cesar Franck (in English)
d'Indy, Vincent: César Franck (in French)
Dianna, B.A.: Benjamin Britten's Holy Theatre
Dolge, Alfred: Pianos and Their Makers. A Comprehensive History
Fischhof, Joseph: Versuch einer Geschichte des Clavierbaues. (Faksimile 1853).
Fuller-Maitland, J.A.: The Music of Parry and Stanford
Geminiani, Francesco: The Art of Playing the Violin.
Häuser: Musikalisches Lexikon. 2 vols in one.
Hawkins, John: A General History of the Science & Practice of Music (5 vols.)
Holmes, Edward: A Ramble among the Musicians of Germany
Hopkins, Antony: The Concertgoer's Companion - Bach to Haydn.
Hopkins, Antony: The Concertgoer's Companion – Holst to Webern.
Hopkins, Antony: Music All Around Me
Hopkins, Antony: Sounds of Music / Sounds of the Orchestra
Hopkins, Antony: The Nine Symphonies of Beethoven
Hopkins, Antony: Understanding Music

Books published by Travis & Emery Music Bookshop:

Hopkins, Edward & Rimboult, Edward: The Organ. Its History & Construction.
Hunt, John: - see separate list of discographies at the end of these titles
Iliffe, Frederick: The Forty-Eight Preludes and Fugues of John Sebastian Bach
Isaacs, Lewis: Hänsel and Gretel. A Guide to Humperdinck's Opera.
Isaacs, Lewis: Königskinder (Royal Children). Guide to Humperdinck's Opera.
Kastner: Manuel Général de Musique Militaire
Kenney, Charles Lamb: A Memoir of Michael William Balfe
Klein, Hermann: Thirty years of musical Life in London, 1870-1900
Lacassagne, M. l'Abbé Joseph : Traité Général des élémens du Chant
Lascelles (née Catley), Anne: The Life of Miss Anne Catley.
McCormack, John: John McCormack: His Own Life Story.
Mainwaring, John: Memoirs of the Life of the Late George Frederic Handel
Malcolm, Alexander: A Treaty of Music: Speculative, Practical and Historical
Manshardt, Thomas: Aspects of Cortot
Marx, Adolph Bernhard: Die Kunst des Gesanges, Theoretisch-Practisch
May, Florence: The Life of Brahms
May, Florence: The Girlhood Of Clara Schumann: Clara Wieck And Her Time.
Mellers, Wilfrid: Angels of the Night: Popular Female Singers of Our Time
Mellers, Wilfrid: Bach and the Dance of God
Mellers, Wilfrid: Beethoven and the Voice of God
Mellers, Wilfrid: Caliban Reborn - Renewal in Twentieth Century Music
Mellers, Wilfrid: Darker Shade of Pale, A Backdrop to Bob Dylan
Mellers, Wilfrid: François Couperin and the French Classical Tradition
Mellers, Wilfrid: Harmonious Meeting
Mellers, Wilfrid: Le Jardin Retrouvé, The Music of Frederic Mompou
Mellers, Wilfrid: Music and Society, England and the European Tradition
Mellers, Wilfrid: Music in a New Found Land: …… American Music
Mellers, Wilfrid: Romanticism and the Twentieth Century (from 1800)
Mellers, Wilfrid: The Masks of Orpheus: …… the Story of European Music.
Mellers, Wilfrid: The Sonata Principle (from c. 1750)
Mellers, Wilfrid: Vaughan Williams and the Vision of Albion
Newmarch, Rosa: Henry J. Wood
Newmarch, Rosa: Jean Sibelius
Newmarch, Rosa: Mary Wakefield, a Memoir
Newmarch, Rosa: The Concert-Goer's Library
Newmarch, Rosa: The Music of Czechoslovakia
Newmarch, Rosa: The Russian Opera.
Nicholas, Jeremy: Godowsky, the Pianists' Pianist
Niecks, Frederick: The Life of Chopin. (2 vols.)

Books published by Travis & Emery Music Bookshop:

Panchianio, Cattuffio: Rutzvanscad Il Giovine
Pearce, Charles: Sims Reeves, Fifty Years of Music in England.
Pepusch, John Christopher: A Treatise on Harmony ...
Pettitt, Stephen: Philharmonia Orchestra: A Record of Achievement, 1948-1985
Pettitt, Stephen (ed. Hunt): Philharmonia Orchestra: Discography 1945-1987
Playford, John: An Introduction to the Skill of Musick.
Porte, John: Sir Charles Villiers Stanford.
Quantz, Johann: Versuch einer Anweisung die Flöte traversiere zu spielen.
Rameau, Jean-Philippe: Code de Musique Pratique, ou Methodes.
Rameau, Jean-Philippe: Erreurs sur La Musique dans l'Encyclopédie
Rastall, Richard: The Notation of Western Music.
Rimbault, Edward: The Pianoforte, Its Origins, Progress, and Construction.
Rousseau, Jean Jacques: Dictionnaire de Musique
Rubinstein, Anton : Guide to the proper use of the Pianoforte Pedals.
Sainsbury, John S.: Dictionary of Musicians. (1825). (2 vols.)
Schumann, Clara & Brahms, Johannes: Letters 1853-1896. (2 vols.)
Scott-Sutherland: Arnold Bax
Serré de Rieux, Jean de : Les dons des Enfans de Latone
Simpson, Christopher: A Compendium of Practical Musick in Five Parts
Smyth, Ethel: Impressions That Remained. (2 vols.)
Spohr, Louis: Autobiography
Spohr, Louis: Grand Violin School
Tans'ur, William: A New Musical Grammar; or The Harmonical Spectator
Terry, Charles Sanford: Bach's Chorals – Parts 1, 2 and 3.
Terry, Charles Sanford: John Christian Bach
Terry, Charles Sanford: J.S. Bach's Original Hymn-Tunes - Congregational Use.
Terry, Charles Sanford: Four-Part Chorals of J.S. Bach. (German & English)
Terry, Charles Sanford: Joh. Seb. Bach, Cantata Texts, Sacred and Secular.
Terry, Charles Sanford: The Origins of the Family of Bach Musicians.
Tosi, Pierfrancesco: Opinioni de' Cantori Antichi, e Moderni
Tosi, Pierfrancesco: Observations on the Florid Song.
Tovey, Donald Francis: A Musician Talks, The Integrity of Music
Tovey, Donald Francis: A Musician Talks, Musical Textures
Tovey, Donald Francis: A Companion to "The Art of the Fugue" J.S. Bach
Tovey, Donald Francis: A Companion to Beethoven's Pianoforte Sonatas
Tovey, Donald Francis: Beethoven
Tovey, Donald Francis: Essays in Musical Analysis. (6 vols.).
Tovey, Donald Francis: The integrity of music
Tovey, Donald Francis: Musical Textures

Books published by Travis & Emery Music Bookshop:

Tovey, Donald Francis: Some English Symphonists
Tovey, Donald Francis: The Main Stream of Music.
Van der Straeten, Edmund: History of the Violoncello, The Viol da Gamba …
Van der Straeten, Edmund: History of the Violin, Its Ancestors… (2 vols.)
Walther, J. G. [Waltern]: Musicalisches Lexikon [Musikalisches Lexicon]
Wagner, Richard: Beethoven (Leipzig 1870)
Wagner, Richard: Lebens-Bericht (Leipzig 1884)
Wagner, Richard: The Musaic of the Future (Translated by E. Dannreuther).
Wyndham, Henry Saxe: The Annals of Covent Garden Theatre. (2 vols.)
Zwirn, Gerald: Stranded Stories From The Operas

Music published by Travis & Emery Music Bookshop:

Bach, Johann Sebastian: Sacred Songs for SCTB, arranged by Franz Wullner.
Bax, Arnold: Symphony #5, Arranged for Piano Four Hands by Walter Emery
Beranger, Pierre Jean de: Musique Des Chansons de Beranger: Airs Notes ...
Bizet, Georges: Djamileh. Vocal Score.
Donizetti, Gaetano: Betly. Dramma Giocoso in Due Atti. Vocal Score.
Frescobaldi, Girolamo: D'Arie Musicali per Cantarsi. Primo & Secondo Libro.
Handel, Purcell, Boyce, Greene ... Calliope or English Harmony: Volume First.
Hopkins, Antony: Sonatine
Purcell, Henry et al: Harmonia Sacra … The First Book, (1726)
Purcell, Henry et al: Harmonia Sacra … Book II (1726)
Sullivan, Arthur Seymour: Ivanhoe. Vocal score.
Sullivan, Arthur Seymour: The Rose of Persia. Vocal Score.
Weckerlin, Jean-Baptiste: Chansons Populaires du Pays de France

Other Books, not on Music:

Anon: A Collection of Testimonies Concerning Several Ministers of the Gospel Amongst People called Quakers, Deceased. [Facsimile of 1760 edn.].
Sandeman-Allen, Arthur: Bee-keeping with Twenty hives.

Available from: Travis & Emery at 17 Cecil Court, London, UK.
(+44) (0) 20 7 240 2129. email on sales@travis-and-emery.com .

Discographies by John Hunt.

3 Italian Conductors and 7 Viennese Sopranos: 10 Discographies: Arturo Toscanini, Guido Cantelli, Carlo Maria Giulini, Elisabeth Schwarzkopf, Irmgard Seefried, Elisabeth Gruemmer, Sena Jurinac, Hilde Gueden, Lisa Della Casa, Rita Streich.

A Gallic Trio: 3 Discographies: Charles Muench, Paul Paray, Pierre Monteux.

A Notable Quartet: 4 Discographies: Gundula Janowitz, Christa Ludwig, Nicolai Gedda, Dietrich Fischer-Dieskau.

American Classics: The Discographies of Leonard Bernstein & Eugene Ormand

Antal Dorati 1906-1988: Discography and Concert Register.

Austro-Hungarian Pianists, Discographies of Lili Kraus, Friedrich Gulda, Ingrid Haebler

Back From The Shadows: 4 Discographies: Willem Mengelberg, Dimitri Mitropoulos, Hermann Abendroth, Eduard Van Beinum.

Carlo Maria Giulini: Discography and Concert Register.

Columbia 33CX Label Discography.

Concert Hall Discography: Concert Hall Society and Concert Hall Record Club

Conductors On The Yellow Label: 8 Discographies: Fritz Lehmann, Ferdinand Leitner, Ferenc Fricsay, Eugen Jochum, Leopold Ludwig, Artur Rother, Franz Konwitschny, Igor Markevitch.

Dirigenten der DDR: Conductors of the German Democratic Republic

Fremd bin ich eingezogen - a critical discography of the piano music of Franz Schubert

From Adam to Webern: the Recordings of von Karajan.

Frosh: Discography of the Richard Strauss Opera Die Frau ohne Schatten

Giants of the Keyboard: 6 Discographies: Wilhelm Kempff, Walter Gieseking, Edwin Fischer, Clara Haskil, Wilhelm Backhaus, Artur Schnabel.

Gramophone Stalwarts: 3 Separate Discographies: Bruno Walter, Erich Leinsdorf, Georg Solti.

Great Violinists: 3 Discographies: David Oistrakh, Wolfgang Schneiderhan, Arthur Grumiaux.

Hans Knappertsbusch: Kna: Concert Register and Discography of Hans Knappertsbusch, 1888-1965. Second Edition.

Her Master's Voice: Concert Register and Discography of Dame Elisabeth Schwarzkopf [Third Edition].

Hungarians in Exile: 3 Discographies: Fritz Reiner, Antal Dorati, George Szell.

Kingsway: Classical Music's Premier Recording Venue.

Leopold Stokowski (1882-1977): Discography and Concert Register

Leopold Stokowski: Discography and Concert Listing.

Leopold Stokowski: Second Edition of the Discography.

Makers of the Philharmonia: 11 Discographies Alceo Galliera, Walter Susskind, Paul Kletzki, Nicolai Malko, Issay Dobrowen, Lovro Von Matacic, Efrem Kurtz, Otto Ackermann, Anatole Fistoulari, George Weldon, Robert Irving.

Metropolitan Sopranos: 4 Discographies: Rosa Ponselle, Eleanor Steber, Zinka Milanov, Leontyne Price.

Mezzo and Contraltos: 5 Discographies: Janet Baker, Margarete Klose, Kathleen Ferrier, Giulietta Simionato, Elisabeth Hoengen.

Mid-Century Conductors and More Viennese Singers: 10 Discographies: Karl Boehm, Victor De Sabata, Hans Knappertsbusch, Tullio Serafin, Clemens Krauss, Anton Dermota, Leonie Rysanek, Eberhard Waechter, Maria Reining, Erich Kunz.

More 20th Century Conductors: 7 Discographies: Eugen Jochum, Ferenc Fricsay, Carl Schuricht, Felix Weingartner, Josef Krips, Otto Klemperer, Erich Kleiber.

More Giants of the Keyboard: 5 Discographies: Claudio Arrau, Gyorgy Cziffra, Vladimir Horowitz, Dinu Lipatti, Artur Rubinstein.

More Musical Knights: 4 Discographies: Hamilton Harty, Charles Mackerras, Simon Rattle, John Pritchard.

Musical Knights: 6 Discographies: Henry Wood, Thomas Beecham, Adrian Boult, John Barbirolli, Reginald Goodall, Malcolm Sargent.

Neglected Instrumentalists: Adrian Aeschbacher, Eduard Erdmann, Conrad Hansen, Ludwig Hoelscher, Georg Kulenkampff, Enrico Mainardi, Carl Seemann, Max Strub, Gerhard Taschner, Friedrich Wührer

Philharmonic Autocrat 1: Discography of: Herbert Von Karajan [3rd Edition]

Philharmonic Autocrat 2: Concert Register of Herbert Von Karajan 2nd. Ed.

Philharmonic Autocrat: Discography of Herbert von Karajan (1908-1989). 4th Ed..

Philharmonisches Orchester Berlin, the historic years, 1913-1954

Philips Minigroove: Second Extended Version of the European Discography.

Pianists For The Connoisseur: 6 Discographies: Arturo Benedetti Michelangeli, Alfred Cortot, Alexis Weissenberg, Clifford Curzon, Solomon, Elly Ney.

Record Pioneers: Richard Strauss, Hans Pfitzner, Oskar Fried, Oswald Kabasta, Karl Muck, Franz Von Hoesslin, Karl Elmendorff.

Sächsische Staatskapelle Dresden: Complete Discography.

Singers of the Third Reich: 5 Discographies: Helge Roswaenge, Tiana Lemnitz, Franz Voelker, Maria Mueller, Max Lorenz.

Singers on the Yellow Label: 7 Discographies: Maria Stader, Elfriede Troetschel, Annelies Kupper, Wolfgang Windgassen, Ernst Haefliger, Josef Greindl, Kim Borg

Six Wagnerian Sopranos: 6 Discographies: Frieda Leider, Kirsten Flagstad, Astrid Varnay, Martha Moedl, Birgit Nilsson, Gwyneth Jones.

Staatskapelle Berlin. The shellac era 1916-1962.

Sviatoslav Richter: Pianist of the Century: Discography.

Teachers and Pupils: 7 Discographies: Elisabeth Schwarzkopf, Maria Ivoguen, Maria Cebotari, Meta Seinemeyer, Ljuba Welitsch, Rita Streich, Erna Berger

Tenors in a Lyric Tradition: 3 Discographies: Peter Anders, Walther Ludwig, Fritz Wunderlich.

The Art of the Diva: 3 Discographies: Claudia Muzio, Maria Callas, Magda Olivero.

The Furtwaengler Sound Sixth Edition: Discography and Concert Listing.

The Furtwängler Sound. Discography of Wilhelm Furtwängler. Seventh Edition.

The Great Dictators: 3 Discographies: Evgeny Mravinsky, Artur Rodzinski, Sergiu Celibidache.

The Lyric Baritone: 5 Discographies: Hans Reinmar, Gerhard Huesch, Josef Metternich, Hermann Uhde, Eberhard Waechter.

The Post-War German Tradition: 5 Discographies: Rudolf Kempe, Joseph Keilberth, Wolfgang Sawallisch, Rafael Kubelik, Andre Cluytens.

Wagner Im Festspielhaus: Discography of the Bayreuth Festival.

Wiener Philharmoniker 1 - Vienna Philharmonic and Vienna State Opera Orchestras: Discography Part 1 1905-1954.

Wiener Philharmoniker 2 - Vienna Philharmonic and Vienna State Opera Orchestras: Discography Part 2 1954-1989.

Wiener Staatsoper: 348 complete relays

Available from: Travis & Emery at 17 Cecil Court, London, UK.
(+44) (0) 20 7 240 2129. email on sales@travis-and-emery.com .

© Travis & Emery 2019

www.ingramcontent.com/pod-product-compliance
Lightning Source LLC
Chambersburg PA
CBHW070356240426
43671CB00013BA/2520